MAVERICK GUIDE TO
BARCELONA

mav-er-ick (mav'er-ik), *n* 1. an unbranded steer. Hence colloq. 2. a person not labeled as belonging to any one faction, group, etc., who acts independently. 3. one who moves in a different direction than the rest of the herd—often a nonconformist. 4. a person using individual judgment, even when it runs against majority opinion.

MAVERICK GUIDE TO
BARCELONA

Richard Schweid

PELICAN PUBLISHING COMPANY
Gretna 1997

Information in this guidebook is based on authoritative data available at the time of printing. Prices and hours of operation of businesses listed are subject to change without notice. Readers are asked to take this into account when consulting this guide.

*Map of the metro system courtesy of Transports Municipales de Barcelona
Other maps courtesy of Turisme de Barcelona*

Manufactured in the United States of America
Published by Pelican Publishing Company, Inc.
1101 Monroe Street, Gretna, Louisiana 70053

Contents

Preface

Barcelona is, above all, a city to be appreciated through the sense of sight. In almost any part of the city, at any time of day or night, one need only look around to find a remarkable vista: a building that takes the breath away with its incredible architecture; a monument that astonishes; the delicate filigree of a wrought iron balcony jutting out over a narrow cobblestoned street; an old man sitting on a bench in a tiny plaza against a backdrop of a church exactly as people have sat in that place since the Middle Ages.

Barcelona has the second largest inhabited medieval neighborhood in Europe, next to Prague, and its narrow, winding streets are an endless joy to walk through. Numerous other neighborhoods offer a wide variety of their own visual pleasures. One does not have to be going anywhere—the simple act of passing through these places is pleasure enough.

Barcelona, like many of the world's greatest cities, is a walker's paradise. Everywhere is reflected the intense concern with form and architecture that has long been a part of the life of its residents. It is a city whose architectural inventory goes through cycles marked by long periods of stasis followed by tremendous changes crammed into the space of a decade or two, after which the city again relaxes for a century or so until a new set of circumstances spark the forces of change and another upheaval occurs. During each of these periods of transformation, intense public debate is sure to accompany the new buildings that appear and the old ones that are destroyed to make room for them. Taxicab drivers, waiters, and hair dressers all have their well-informed opinions on the city's latest architectural changes.

The Summer Olympics of 1992 was one of those periods of renaissance. Once Barcelona's selection as an Olympic city was officially announced in 1986, a veritable fever of demolition and construction seized the city. Projects that had been discussed, postponed, discussed, and postponed again, many times over, suddenly took shape. Blueprints were hauled out of filing cabinets where they had been gathering dust for years, funds were found, and the face of the city began to be drastically altered. A decade later, in

1996, the city had been profoundly changed. While each new step drew its critics, it was generally conceded that most of the changes had been for the better and that the city had been greatly improved.

Many of these changes work to the direct benefit of visitors. There are almost two miles of open Mediterranean beach along the edge of downtown Barcelona, where before there were warehouses and railroad tracks. Many parts of the city have been made accessible which were previously difficult to reach. A great deal of money was spent on improving the city's transportation. Thousands of cab drivers and shopkeepers took English lessons. There are many more parks and open spaces where people can relax, and a new pride on the part of the city's residents that theirs is a city that is immensely attractive to foreigners.

Barcelona is a pleasure to walk through and observe, but it is also much more. The city is often called the artistic and intellectual capital of Spain. It has numerous cultural attractions and a nightlife that is generally regarded as one of the most exciting in Europe. In addition, the cuisine of Barcelona has been seriously underrated in the past. It is comprised of a wide variety of fresh ingredients brought together in a most delightful manner, and good food is available on almost every block.

This is the city that is considered to be the most "European" in Spain. It is the most cultured and cosmopolitan on the Iberian peninsula, a crossroads between Spain and the rest of the continent. In addition, it is first and foremost the capital of Catalunya, the most northeasterly province of Spain with a population of about six million people. It has its own language—Catalan—that is older than Castilian, which is what the rest of the world knows as Spanish. While the traditional English spelling of the region's name is Catalonia, this book will refer to it as its citizens do: Catalunya.

Many foreigners assume that the Catalan language is nothing more than a dialect of Castilian, but should they mention this to a Catalan person they quickly learn they are mistaken. It is a different language, made up of words that are related to French and Italian as well as Spanish. During the nearly forty years that Francisco Franco Bahamonde ruled Spain with his dictator's iron fist—1939-1975—Catalan was a forbidden language and the people of Catalunya were required to speak only Castilian. Only behind closed doors did families talk in Catalan. The struggle between Franco and the Catalans was fierce, in part because Catalunya was the last area to surrender to Franco's forces during the Spanish Civil War and offered the most spirited resistance.

For an excellent and readable account of Barcelona and the Spanish during the Civil War, read George Orwell's *Homage to Catalonia,* describing his experiences as a soldier fighting for the Republic. When Barcelona fell to the Falangists on Jan. 2, 1939, the war was, for all intents and purposes, over.

Franco never forgot nor forgave the Catalan resistance. When he died on Nov. 20, 1975, the ancient Catalan language rapidly reappeared in public. Having been prohibited for so long from speaking it, the Catalans find the liberty to do so understandably important. It is every bit as important to them as French is to someone from Quebec. For an excellent Catalan history and essay on contemporary life, read *Barcelona,* by Robert Hughes. For a journalistic portrait of contemporary Barcelona, read my own book: *Barcelona: Jews, Transvestites, and an Olympic Season.*

Today, Catalunya has two official languages: Castilian and Catalan. There are films, plays, books, newspapers, and television channels in Catalan. Children in school learn both Catalan and Castilian. Street and place names in this book will be given in Catalan, because that is how they are most often encountered. Many street names read like this: Carrer de Casanova, which would be Calle de Casanova in Castilian, or Casanova Street in English. In this book, such street names will be rendered C de Casanova. For *avinguda,* the Catalan for avenue, I'll use Av.

While the issue of language is one that excites heated debate and high passions here, the passer-through need not worry about it. Catalans will generally respond to any attempt to communicate on the part of foreigners. And with the recent popularity of English lessons, many of them can speak that language—at least on a rudimentary level. Barcelona hosts millions of tourists each year and you are not likely to be the first of the species being encountered by any given Barcelona resident. If you don't speak Spanish, you may find someone who speaks a little English, or be able to communicate in basic sign language. Most Barcelonese do not mind, and will attempt to communicate back to you in whichever language you attempt.

The glossary of terms and sample menu in the back of this book are written in Castilian and Catalan. Catalans do not expect that people from other places will communicate with them in their regional language. Catalan is spoken only by a few million people, 99.9 percent of them in one small part of the world. Castilian is the native tongue of over 300 million, and it will serve you as well in Barcelona as it will in Bogota or Buenos Aires. Visitors who are looking forward to using their Spanish can rest assured that all Catalans do speak Castilian, and anyone who speaks Spanish as we know it to a Catalan person will be understood and almost always answered in kind.

The struggle between Franco and the Catalans was by no means the first conflict between a central government in Madrid and the region of Catalunya. In the Middle Ages, Catalunya was part of the kingdon of Aragon and found itself frequently struggling with Castile. In fact, as the historical record shows, such struggles have been the single largest determining factor in the history of Catalunya and Barcelona, and they continue to be so today.

A Little History. 218 B.C.: Barcelona founded by the Carthaginians, named Barcino after Hamilcar Barca, father of the famous Carthaginian general Hannibal.

100 B.C.: The Carthaginians, having lost the Second Punic War to the Romans, are expelled from Barcelona and all of Catalunya. The Romans establish their capital in Tarragona but Barcelona continues to thrive.

415 A.D.: The Romans lose Catalunya to the Visigoths, who make Barcelona their capital for a brief time before moving on and leaving the city behind to slumber in relative unimportance for the next four centuries.

713: Barcelona falls to the Moors from North Africa who have been moving steadily northward through Spain. They rename the city Bargelona in Arabic.

801: The Moors lose Barcelona, after less than a century, to Charlemagne's forces, the Franks. A count is established in the city whose main responsibility is to defend the area against Moors. This signals a period of growth and expansion for Catalunya, which begins to come into its own with a series of counts at its head who have their seats of power in Barcelona, starting with Guifré el Pilós (Wilfred the Hairy), the first count of Barcelona.

1137: Catalunya and Aragon become unified. This presages the beginning of the Golden Age for Catalunya and Barcelona, which have an economic and political influence that extends throughout the Mediterranean.

1289: Jaume I founds Catalunya's parliament and the generalitat to govern the region.

1391: Riots during the summer wipe out the city's Jewish population, predating by a century the 1492 expulsion of all Jews from Spain.

1412: A Castilian prince, Ferdinand de Antequera, is elected to the Catalan throne. By the end of the century, Spain has become united under the "Catholic Monarchs," Ferdinand (this one from Aragon) and Isabella. With their focus on exploration, they remove power, influence, and wealth from Catalunya, which is forbidden to participate in the plundering of the New World and must content itself with a much diminished Mediterranean commerce. For the next two centuries, Catalunya chafes under the administration of a series of viceroys who put increasing limits on Catalan autonomy and independence.

1635: Catalunya declares its independence from Spain and begins its rebellion against the forces of Madrid, asking Louis XIII of France for aid and protection. However, seventeen years later, Catalunya surrenders to the Spanish army. In 1659 Spain and France sign an agreement that cedes part of Catalunya, the area around Perpignan, to France. "Els Segadors" ("The Reapers") was the marching song of this war and became the Catalan national anthem.

1700: When Charles II dies without leaving an heir, the War of the Spanish Succession begins. Castile accepts Louis XIV's grandson, Phillip II of France, as the king, but Catalunya and all the territories of the former kingdom of Aragon support Archduke Charles of Austria, who has promised he will support their autonomy.

1714: Barcelona holds out, fighting a lone battle against the repressive policies of the Bourbon king, Phillip V, who closed the university and banned the use of the Catalan language. They are the last Catalans to resist. They surrender on September 11, 1714, the date that is still Catalunya's "national" holiday.

1800-1850: Catalunya recovers its economic health and prominence, becoming the first of Spain's regions to enter the modern industrial age and construct large factories. In addition, as of 1778, they are authorized, finally, to do trade with the Americas.

1855: The walls of the old Bourbon city are demolished and Ildefons Cerda i Sunyer begins drawing up plans to expand the city, which results in the Eixample.

1909: The *setmana tràgica* ("tragic week") takes place in the month of July, when riots break out in the streets over the Madrid government's demand that people serve in troops to go fight in Morocco. Rampant inflation drives many people from the countryside to the city, and Barcelona doubles its size during the first 20 years of the century. The anarchist worker's union has a half million members in Catalunya, and Barcelona is a hotbed of radical politics.

1923: A military coup by Primo de Rivera establishes a fascist dictatorship that prohibits any degree of autonomy for Catalunya.

1930: The Depression forces de Rivera to resign and the Second Republic is elected. In Catalunya, the election winners are leftists headed by Francesc Macià, who initially declares Catalunya's full independence, then agrees to remain within the Spanish Republic as an autonomous region. The Generalitat is reestablished with far-reaching administrative powers.

July 18, 1936: General Francisco Franco, stationed in Morocco, leads an uprising of troops against the Republic, beginning a war that does not end until January 1939, and that will leave two million Spaniards dead and millions more in exile.

Jan. 2, 1939: Barcelona is the last city in Spain to surrender to Franco's forces. Its capitulation ushers in 36 years of dictatorship during which Catalan is strictly forbidden, as are any expressions of the Catalan culture.

Nov. 20, 1975: Franco dies and Spain begins its transformation into a democracy. King Juan Carlos I assumes the throne. Autonomy begins to be reinstated in Catalunya.

March 1980: First Catalan elections held.

Feb. 23, 1981: An attempted coup by members of the military and the national police force fails when the king refuses to endorse the attempt. The plotters are arrested and democracy continues.

March 1982: Felipe Gonzalez and his Socialist party win an absolute majority in the Congress.

July-August 1992: The 1992 Summer Olympics are held in Barcelona and provide the city with a reason to rebuild its infrastructure and prepare for the 21st century.

March 1996: The *Partido Popular* ("Popular Party") narrowly wins national elections. This center-right party comes to power with Jose María Aznar as the new prime minister, while Gonzalez and his fellow socialists take up the role of the opposition. Aznar forms an alliance with the Catalan nationalist party in order to have a majority in parliament, thereby providing Catalunya and its president Jordi Pujol with a tremendous amount of power on the national political stage.

Introduction

Among the qualities ascribed to Catalans by other Spaniards—to which Catalans will admit—are that they are harder-working, more concerned with material possessions, thriftier, less spontaneous, and more European than people from the rest of the country. There are, however, also many things that they share with other Spaniards, and some of these will be the first to impress foreigners.

One, and perhaps the most difficult, component of Spanish life to which tourists will have to adjust is the hours that Spaniards keep. Jet lag wears off after a few days, and the change in time zones is rapidly adapted to by our bodies, but our eating and sleeping habits are deeply ingrained and changing them can be difficult. It is not easy for North Americans to get used to eating lunch at 2:30 P.M. and dinner at 10 P.M., and going out to hear music in a nightclub when the first set does not begin until after midnight. Nevertheless, be prepared. Most restaurants simply will not serve dinner, for instance, before 8:30 P.M. at the earliest. If you go out to a concert, it may not begin until 10 P.M., and nightclubs do not begin to fill up until around 1 A.M. This much is empirical data. How the locals manage to do it and also attend to family, business, and sleep remains something of a mystery.

Then, there is the question of the Spanish work schedule. It goes something like this: Get to work at 9 A.M., go for a coffee and a bite to eat at 11, come back at 11:30, go for the midday meal at 2 P.M., come back at 4:30, and work until 8, with maybe a little break for a snack around 6:30. Another schedule change to be aware of is that during the summer, many businesses adopt "summer hours," which means they are open from 8 A.M.-3 P.M. and closed for the rest of the day.

It is not just *yanquis* ("yankees") who have trouble with the Spanish schedule. It has caused great consternation among members of the European Union. In Britain or France, the workday more closely resembles that of the States, and when a businessman in London or Paris cannot find a Spaniard in his office between 2 and 4:30 P.M. it makes things difficult. Nevertheless, the Spaniards are resisting calls for change from their trading partners, and

15

while their schedule is modifying ever so slowly, visitors need to be prepared. A good training schedule for the month before you leave is to eat dinner a few minutes later each night and go to bed a little later also.

In the days of Franco, travelers came to Spain and Barcelona because of the cheap prices. Not any longer. While Barcelona is not terribly expensive by European standards, its prices can certainly shock Americans. It has been many years since Spain was a destination for bargain travelers, and visitors to Barcelona should expect prices to resemble those of any large, first-world city.

Barcelona is neither excessively clean nor excessively dirty. There are large green garbage containers for residential trash and garbage on every corner, and within the last few years the city has begun an ambitious recycling program, putting glass, tin, and paper recycling bins on the corners of many blocks. It is, unfortunately, still necessary to take time out from looking up at the beautiful buildings to scan the sidewalks for dog droppings. The Barcelonese are great dog lovers, and there are no municipal restrictions on cleaning up after man's best friend, so pedestrians need to beware or they will spend a lot of time scraping the soles of their shoes clean.

This is one of the most densely populated cities in the world. About 1.5 million people live in about 40 square miles (the population of Barcelona when its suburbs are included is over 3 million) bounded by hills and sea. On certain days, the air can be heavy with exhaust fumes, thick, and not pleasant to breathe. Then, a strong breeze will come off the sea, or down from the hills, and each breath will be clean, sharp, and refreshing. On a clear day, Barcelona gleams.

Standard security precautions apply to life here. While the city is exceptionally safe by North American standards—there are almost no random murders on the streets and pistols are extremely difficult for the average citizen to obtain—robbery at knifepoint happens occasionally, particularly in some of the rundown areas of the old city late at night. In addition, pickpockets abound, particularly during tourist season at those spots favored by visitors, and in the last few years this kind of crime has seen a marked rise.

Commonsense measures help greatly: do not sit at an outdoor café and put your purse or briefcase in an empty seat next to you, because some fleet-footed youth may come by and grab it. Do not carry a lot of money late at night. It is the law that everyone must carry identification, but be prudent by carrying a photocopy of the front page of your passport and leaving the real thing in the safe deposit box at your hotel. While belly-packs have the disadvantage of marking you as a probable tourist, they make it harder to lose documents or cash to pickpockets. In case you do fall victim to such a crime, contact the police and your local consulate.

Barcelona's location, alone, makes it a joy to visit. It is built between the Mediterranean and a range of high hills called the Collserola. Travel two hours north and you reach the Pyrenees, with some of the best skiing this side of the Alps. Three hours south and you are in Valencia, the land of sunshine and oranges.

THE CONFESSIONAL

Unlike many other guidebooks, this one contains no advertising, either overt or covert. The opinions expressed—and there are many—are mine. As with other books in the series, no one can use friendship or favors to influence the coverage of personal commercial interests. You may not agree with my opinion, but you will know that it is based on my personal experience and is given openly and honestly.

It has not been possible to stay in every hotel that a visitor can use, but the book covers a good range from luxury to basic. Likewise with restaurants and shops—you will end up eating at, or visiting, some places not mentioned in this publication. If they are particularly good, cheap, friendly, or interesting, please let me know about them so that I can visit them before completing the next edition of the guide.

GETTING THE MOST OUT OF THIS BOOK

This guide is arranged in a pattern similar to that of the other Maverick Guides. It is a tried and tested format that has been used since the 1980s and it enables you to get a good feel for the city and its people while at the same time getting the specifics that are so necessary when you are traveling.

After a chapter on how to reach Barcelona, how to travel around when you arrive, and how to smooth the basics of government requirements and travel practicalities, there is an overview chapter on the city, and then specific area chapters. The chapters need not be read in that sequence, of course. However, if you are using the book to plan your trip, I suggest that you read all sections so that you can decide which areas to visit.

Each of the area chapters is divided into seven numbered parts, and after you become familiar with them in one chapter, you will know where to look for these same subjects in each of the other chapters. The categories are as follows:

1. **Orientation**
2. **The Hotel Scene**
3. **Restaurants and Cafés**
4. **Sightseeing**
5. **Sports**
6. **Shopping**
7. **Nightlife and Entertainment**

The book has been set up to be used in two ways. First, you should look through it thoroughly before you leave home. Make some plans on the basis of this reading. Decide where you would like to visit and what you would like to do when you are there. Select some hotels, determine if there are some specific restaurants that you will visit, consider which tours have appeal, and make a list of the things you would like to buy while in Barcelona. Then go and talk to your travel agent. Remember that while travel agents are well qualified to advise on airfares and some package tours, it is unrealistic to expect them to be familiar with details of all destinations around the world. A good agent will appreciate your making informed suggestions and will benefit from the contact names and telephone numbers found inside this guide.

The book is also designed to be used when you are in Barcelona. The recommendations on sightseeing tours, hotels, restaurants, and shopping will help you in your quest for smooth, fun traveling. The information on sightseeing will help broaden your horizons and encourage you to explore things that most visitors miss. All the sections will help you save time and money as you travel through Barcelona.

MAVERICK GUIDE TO
BARCELONA

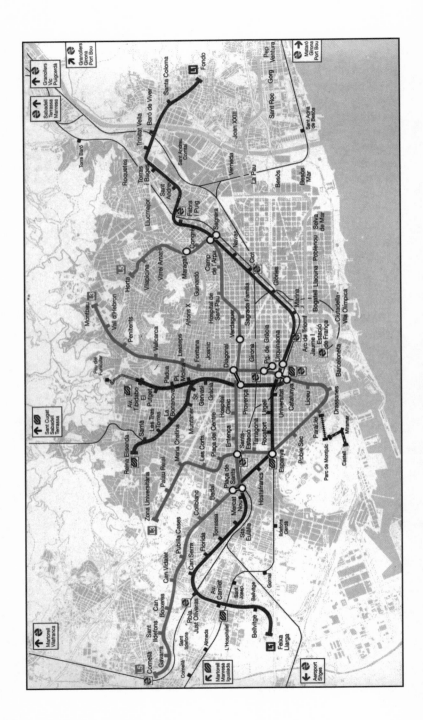

1

How to Get
the Best from Barcelona:
Practical Tips

Before You Leave

The **Spanish Tourist Office** can provide you with a good deal of useful information about Barcelona before you begin your trip. They have all kinds of basic information for the asking.

The Spanish Tourist Office has offices in Chicago at Water Tower Place, Suite 915 East, 845 Michigan Ave., Chicago IL 60611 (Tel. 312-944-0216); Los Angeles at 8383 Wilshire Blvd., Suite 960, Beverly Hills, CA 90211 (Tel. 213-658-7188); Miami at 1221 Brickell Ave., Miami, FL 33131 (Tel. 305-358-1992); New York City at 665 Fifth Ave., New York, NY 10022 (Tel. 212-759-8822); Toronto at 102 Bloor St. West, 14th Floor, Toronto, Ontario M5S1M8, Canada (Tel. 416-961-3131); London at 57-58 St. James St., London SW 1A 1LD, England (Tel. 499-1169); and Sydney at 203 Castlereagh St., Level 2, P.O. Box A-685, Sydney NSW 2000, Australia (Tel. 264-7966). In addition, there is a Catalonia Tourism Board office in London at Halliburton House, 5 Putney Bridge Approach, London SW6 3GD, England (Tel. 371-0233).

Eurail Information. This can be obtained from Rail Europe, P.O. Box 10383, Stamford, CT 06904.

Visas, Passports, and Inoculations. For travelers from the U.S. or Canada who are planning to stay in Spain less than three months, no visa is necessary. Inoculations are not necessary unless you are coming from an infected area. It usually takes about three weeks to obtain a U.S. passport. First-time U.S. passport applicants require 1) proof of citizenship; 2) two passport photographs; 3) proof of identity (such as an official copy of your birth certificate); 4) a fee of $65 for those over 18 and $42 for those under 18; and 5) an application form available from a federal passport agency, a post office or a courthouse. A passport is valid for 10 years from date of issue.

Driver's License. You must carry a valid driver's license from your country of origin to drive in Barcelona. An international driver's license is not required, and a driver's license from another country is legally valid here for a year. After that you're supposed to have a local driver's license.

Getting There

BY AIR

The approach by air is lovely, over long stretches of beach. Barcelonese concern for architecture is evident to visitors as soon as they deplane at the **Aeroport del Prat,** located seven miles outside Barcelona on the highway to Castelldefels and Sitges. The airport's international terminal with its walls of glass, marble floors, and artificial, lifelike palm trees inside was designed by Ricard Bofill, one of the city's premiere architects, and opened in 1991 in anticipation of the Olympics.

International flights are rarely cheap, but there is a great variety in prices depending on the time of year one travels and where the ticket is purchased. Consolidators, referred to in the trade as "bucket shops," advertise in the Sunday editions of large metropolitan newspapers like the *New York Times* and frequently offer tickets on regular airlines at half the price of a regular travel agent.

Only **TWA** and **Delta,** of all the stateside airlines, offer direct flights to Barcelona from the U.S. Delta's departs from Atlanta and TWA's from New York's Kennedy airport. **Iberia** (Spain's national airline) offers a direct flight from New York, or Miami with a stop in Madrid, as does British Airways. Most of the world's other major airlines also fly into Barcelona. Because routes and companies change, it is always advisable for travelers or their agents to check the current alignment.

Airport Transportation. A taxi ride to the center of Barcelona will cost about 2,300 pesetas ($19 at 1996 exchange rates) from the airport. While this is a fairly modest price, travelers without much luggage may prefer to avail themselves of the comfortable **Aerobús** that leaves the airport every 15 minutes and terminates its run in the Plaça de Catalunya. The fare is 420 pesetas and the bus makes the following stops coming from the airport: Plaça d'Espanya, Estacià de Sants, Av. Roma/Urgell, C de Consell de Cent/Passeig de

Gràcia, and the Plaça de Catalunya. When going to the airport, the order of stops will be reversed. The bus does not stop anywhere else, but if one of these is a convenient stop for you, it is well worth considering. Travelers may be able to save some money by going from the airport to the Plaça de Catalunya by Aerobús, then going on to their final destination by taxi, bus, or metro (subway)—all of which are accessible from the plaça.

The Aerobús leaves the Plaça de Catalunya for the airport every 15 minutes between 5:30 A.M. and 10 P.M. Mon.-Fri. and every 30 minutes from 6 A.M. to 10 P.M. on Sat., Sun., and holidays. It leaves from the airport every 15 minutes from 6 A.M. to 11 P.M. Mon.-Fri., and every 30 minutes from 6:30 A.M. to 10:30 P.M. on Sat., Sun., and holidays. There are also trains to the airport from the train station at Sants, leaving Mon.-Fri. every 30 minutes between 5:44 A.M. and 10:14 P.M., but it's a slow ride. Unless you happen to be staying right next to the Sants train station, the Aerobús is a better idea.

BY TRAIN

RENFE is the Spanish railroad, serving both national and international destinations. For people traveling to Barcelona from another point in Spain, the train will arrive at the **Estació de Sants** at the end of the Av. Roma in the Plaça Paisos Catalan. For those arriving from an international point of origin, the train arrives at the **Estació de França,** Av. Marquès de l'Argentera, s/n ("s/n" means *sin numero,* i.e., without a street number).

Both stations have luggage lockers, money exchange facilities, and showers for passengers. National and international tickets can be purchased in either station. Tickets can also be bought by phone and delivered to a home or hotel room, if they are ordered twenty-four hours in advance and you are willing to pay the fee for a messenger service (this fee should be under $10 during weekday business hours).

The station at Sants also has a tourist office open Mon.-Fri. from 8 A.M. to 8 P.M. and on Sat., Sun., and holidays from 8 A.M. to 2 P.M. There is also a bank of telephones with an operator where travelers may make long-distance phone calls or send a fax and pay for them on the spot. This is open from 8 A.M. to 10:45 P.M. Mon.-Fri.

For information on trains within Spain call 490-0202 between 7 A.M. and 10:30 P.M. seven days a week. For information about international trains call 490-1122, Mon.-Fri., 10 A.M.-2 P.M. and 4-8 P.M.

RENFE offers a number of discount tickets including those for children and people over sixty; for groups of more than six people; and for people traveling on long-distance trains running during off-peak hours Mon.-Thur. and on Saturdays.

Other discounts are also available. There is a **Tourist Railcard** for people who live outside of Spain. This can be obtained at the Sants station by showing a passport and allows you to get three days of unlimited rail travel in one month for 15,400 ptas. in second class and 19,800 ptas. in first class. Also available for higher prices are five-and ten-day tickets.

International discounts for people under 26 are available through **Wasteel** and **Eurotren.** These tickets are valid for two months and are discounted up to 40 percent depending on the destination. Wasteel has an office in the Sants station (Tel.: 490-3929) and Eurotren tickets can be bought at the office of student tourism, C Calabria, 147 (Tel.: 483-8383). In addition, RENFE honors Eurail passes and Eurail Youth passes.

There is a metro station in the Sants station and buses and taxis are at hand just outside. Buses and cabs are available outside the Estació de França.

BY CAR

There are two principal ways to come into Barcelona by car. One is from the south and one is from the north. As in any large city, it is best to avoid driving into the city during the morning rush hour and leaving during the evening.

In addition, Barcelona is notorious for the length of its traffic jams going out of the city on Friday evening and, particularly, coming back to the city on Sunday evening. It can take hours to cover the last fifteen kilometers into Barcelona on a Sunday evening in the early summer when everyone is returning from a weekend at the coast, or during the winter when people are coming back from a ski weekend in the Pyrenees.

BY BUS

Riding a bus between cities or countries in Europe is a lot more pleasant than doing the same thing in the U.S. Buses in Spain have high, clean windows to look out of, and comfortable seats, and they show on-board movies to while away the time.

A few buses still arrive in the back of the Sants train station, but most come to Barcelona's new bus station, **Estació de Autobusos Barcelona Nord,** 80 C de Ali-bei. This is close to the Arc de Triomf and the Ciutadella Park. The metro station is Arc de Triomf (L-1, the red line), and city bus number 54 also terminates here.

Tickets for both national and international destinations can be bought in the station. There are luggage lockers and a money changing facility. Different destinations are served by different bus lines. The main telephone number for the bus station is 265-6508 and you can call between 7 A.M. and 9 P.M.

BY SHIP

Transmediterránea, the national passenger ship company, offers service between Barcelona and the Balearic islands, the Canary islands, Cádiz,

Valencia, Málaga, Almería, and Algeciras, as well as the North African ports of Ceuta and Melilla. Tickets can be bought at the port office, Moll de Barcelona (Tel.: 443-2532).

Barcelona Information

There are four Barcelona tourist offices open year-round. The one in the Estació de Sants is open Mon.-Fri. from 8 A.M. to 8 P.M. and Sat., Sun., and holidays from 8 A.M. to 2 P.M. It is closed on Dec. 25 and 26, Jan. 1, and Jan. 6, which is the Day of the Three Kings in Spain and which many people consider more important than Christmas Day.

There is also a tourist information office in the airport, which is open Mon.-Sat., 9:30 A.M.-8:30 P.M., and on Sun. and holidays, 9:30 A.M.-3 P.M. (Tel. 478-4704). The tourist office for Barcelona and Catalunya (Tel. 304-3134) is in the Plaça de Catalunya, across from the El Corte Inglés department store, which also offers a money-changing facility. It is open 9 A.M.-9 P.M. all year, with the exception of Dec. 25 and 26, Jan. 1, and Jan. 6.

From the end of June until the end of September there are also tourist information booths at the Sagrada Familia church and at the port. In addition, during this time, there are a number of students who are hired during the summer to walk through the streets of the old city in pairs, wearing red jackets and a badge with an *i* for information on it. They speak English and will be glad to assist tourists who have questions.

For those situations in which help is needed immediately—police, medical, or legal advice, and any other emergency—there is a Tourist Attention Service, at La Rambla, 43, open during the winter from 7 A.M. to midnight, and summer from 7 A.M. to 2 A.M., seven days a week (Tel.: 301-9060).

Airline Information. The main offices of the transatlantic airlines serving Barcelona, with addresses and phone numbers, are listed below:

Aerolineas Argentinas	634 Gran Via de les Corts Catalanes	430-5880
Air France	63 Pg. de Gràcia	487-2526
Alitalia	403 Av. Diagonal	416-0424
British Airways	85 Pg. de Gràcia	487-2112
Delta Airlines	16 Pg. de Gràcia, 5°B	412-4333
Iberia	30 Pg. de Gràcia	401-3382
KLM	Barcelona Airport	379-5458
Lufthansa	55 Pg. de Gràcia	487-0300
Swissair	44 Pg. de Gràcia, 2°	215-9100
TAP, Air Portugal	272 C de Mallorca	215-6565
TWA	55 Pg. de Gràcia	215-8188

Foreign Investor Information. Those interested in investment possibilities in Barcelona should contact the **Cambra de Comerç** (the "Chamber of Commerce"), 452 Av. Diagonal (Tel.: 416-9300; Fax: 416-0984).

City Maps. The best place to buy a city map is at any news kiosk, where they carry easy-to-use maps of Barcelona in a variety of languages. They come with a little booklet that lists the streets and gives you the coordinates on the map. When buying the map, be careful not to lose that little booklet, or the map will lose a considerable amount of its value to you. While free tourist brochures often have partial maps, the few dollars needed to buy a map at a kiosk are money well-spent.

When to Visit

Barcelona is a city that has something to offer visitors at any time of the year. Perhaps the worst time for seeing normal life in Barcelona is during August. It is hot and the city is virtually shut down. Most working Spaniards get a month's vacation every year, and most of them have to take that month in August, so the city comes to a standstill. Many of the people in the streets in August are from somewhere else, or they are Barcelonese who are too poor to get out of town.

Still, those businesses that are open welcome your trade in August. And, right smack dab in the middle of the month is the festival of the **Gràcia** neighborhood, which lasts a whole week, and is immediately followed by a festival in the **Sants** neighborhood. Both feature competitions between the various blocks in the neighborhood to decorate the streets and the results are lots of fun to walk through. There is also a good deal of live music outdoors each night, and many activities during the day, including a number of things oriented toward younger children. Gràcia is one of the city's most interesting residential neighborhoods, traditionally a place for young, hip types to live, and is well worth a visit even when there's not a festival.

July is often hot, but there is also the **Festival Grec** ("Greek Festival"), which brings numerous cultural events to town, including concerts by people known worldwide, theatre events, and exhibitions of art and photography. The beaches are crowded and people are outdoors until late at night.

September is a wonderful month to come to Barcelona. The weather has cooled down and everyone is back from vacation, relaxed and anticipating the year ahead. The middle of September marks the beginning of the week-long **Feste de la Mercè,** the festival of Our Lady of Mercy. This is the most important local holiday of the year. There are free concerts each night at various points around town, as well as parades, folk dancing, wine and food fairs, competitions of *castellers* (human pyramids consisting of boys standing on the shoulders of men with even younger boys standing on their shoulders), a *Correfoc* ("fire run") in which fireworks-spewing dragons and devils chase crowds down the broad Via Laietana during a wild and exciting night, and a final huge display of fireworks over the port on the final night.

Like September, the month of May has much to recommend a visit. Air fares are not yet at their summer levels and the weather is often exceptional.

For those who like to ski, a winter trip to Barcelona can be rewarding. The city does not get really cold—temperatures virtually never fall below freezing—and the Pyrenees can be reached in a couple of hours.

Public Holidays. The following are public holidays with the dates they were celebrated in 1996: New Year's Day (Jan. 1); Day of the Kings (Jan. 6); Day of St. Joseph (March 19); Good Friday (April 1); Easter Monday (April 4); Whitsuntide (May 23); Day of Saint John (June 24); The Assumption (August 15); Catalunya Day (La Diada on Sept. 11); Day of La Mercè (Sept. 24); Day of the Spanish Speaking Nations (Oct. 12); All Saints Day (Nov. 1); Day of the Constitution (Dec. 6); Day of the Immaculate Conception (Dec. 8); Christmas Day (Dec. 25); and Boxing Day (Dec. 26).

Spain is a wonderful country for festivals, and Barcelona features a number of nice ones. In addition to La Mercè, there is the **Cavalcada de Reis** ("Cavalcade of Kings") on Jan. 5, a procession of floats featuring the three kings come from afar that makes its way from the waterfront to Montjuïc. Next comes the run-up to the **setmana santa** ("Holy Week"), which is called **Carnaval**. It begins on **Dijous Gras** ("Fat Thursday") and continues with some pretty raucous carryings-on in the way of parades and costume balls until the following Wednesday, Ash Wednesday. On April 23 is the **Festa de Sant Jordi** ("Feast of Saint George," the patron saint of Catalunya). The traditional way of honoring the day is for men to give women flowers and women to give men books. This is not a holiday off from work, but it is traditionally a relaxed day, when the streets are filled with women carrying bouquets and men with a book under their arms. Florists and book sellers move their wares out to the sidewalk, weather permitting, and do a brisk business. Then, in late June, there is the nighttime revel of the **Festa de Sant Joan** ("Feast of Saint John"), when bonfires are lit on street corners and fireworks go off all night long. It's a night for people to get together and celebrate.

Climate. Barcelona enjoys a mild, Mediterranean climate, and each season has its attractions. Spring and fall are mild and lovely, and as summer approaches so does beach weather. Winter, while mild by northern standards, can be cool and wet, and many of the turn-of-the-century, high-ceilinged Barcelona apartments can be damp and cold. Nevertheless, winter is always punctuated with stretches of warm weather, and as the Christmas season approaches, the streets and shops take on a particularly festive air. Average temperature and precipitation by month are listed below:

	Avg. Temperature		Avg. Rainfall	
Jan.	50 F	10 C	1.7 in	.4.4 cm.
Feb.	56 F	13 C	1.4 in.	3.6 cm.
March	56 F	13 C	1.9 in.	4.8 cm.
April	57 F	14 C	2.0 in.	5.1 cm.
May	65 F	18 C	2.3 in.	5.7 cm.
June	70 F	21 C	1.5 in.	3.8 cm.
July	78 F	25 C	0.9 in.	2.2 cm.
Aug.	78 F	25 C	2.6 in.	6.6 cm.
Sept.	72 F	22 C	3.1 in.	7.9 cm.
Oct.	65 F	18 C	3.7 in.	9.4 cm.
Nov.	61 F	16 C	2.9 in.	7.4 cm.
Dec.	54 F	12 C	2.0 in.	5.0 cm.

Do not forget that these are averages, taken over numerous years; the daily temperatures can be expected to vary substantially, as can the monthly rainfalls.

Where to Stay

Hotels. As in most of Europe, the hotels in Barcelona are graded, receiving from one to five stars according to the judgment of inspectors from the Generalitat de Catalunya. The Generalitat also publishes a booklet, *Hoteles, Campings, Apartamentos,* which contains a good listing of the establishments in the title, with prices and amenities offered. It is available from the tourist office at 658 Gran Via de les Corts Catalanes. Some of the better hotels have 800 numbers for making reservations from the States, and all can be booked by a fax from you or your travel agent before you leave home. Reservations are highly recommended. For those who arrive without them, a room of some sort, somewhere, can almost always be found, but the search may be long and arduous, particularly on the heels of a tiresome journey. A number of the smaller, less expensive hotels have a faithful clientele that stay with them each year, and as a result they have only a limited number of rooms available during busy seasons.

At the end of 1995, the city had almost 15,000 hotel rooms available in some 160 hotels. Room prices quoted here are from the Barcelona sales guide for 1996, published by the city's tourist bureau. The rates have been converted using an exchange rate of 125 ptas. to the dollar. They range from plush to bare and everything in between. Unless it's a slow season, hotel prices have a way of going up every few years, and the dollar tends to fluctuate against the peseta, so it's always best to check in advance, or at least allow for the possibility that prices will be higher than listed here.

Hotels listed as offering business conveniences have meeting rooms, fax machines, someone on staff who speaks English, express checkout, etc. All the hotels listed have private baths, central air and heat, telephones, in-room televisions with satellite reception, and private parking unless otherwise noted.

As elsewhere, hotels in Barcelona may add high surcharges when you phone from your room. It is always best to ask at the desk whether there are surcharges for either local or long-distance calls so you won't be surprised by substantial additions to your bill when you check out. When a hotel doesn't have private parking, you will have to use one of Barcelona's many public parking garages, which can cost between $15 and $25 per day.

Youth Hostels. There are a number of them, mostly concentrated around the **Plaça Reial**. They sleep at least four to a room, often more, and are reasonably priced ($10-15 a night) and centrally located. You will meet young and not-so-young people from all over the world in Barcelona's youth hostels. Security is not necessarily at the level of a hotel, so be extra careful with your belongings.

Among the most popular youth hostels are:

Alberg Juvenil Kabul, 17 Plaça Reial (Tel. 318-5190, Fax 301-4034).There is a constant party in progress here once the sun goes down, and there is loud music in the game room, which features a bar, pool tables, and a satellite television. There are 150 beds in double, triple, and quadruple rooms, as well as dormitories, and they are frequently full.

Hostal de Joves Internacional Colon III, 3 C de Colom (Tel. 318-0631).This place, located between Plaça Reial and La Rambla, has 100 beds in a variety of rooms, including dormitory-style. It is not a place to go to get away from it all, as a party atmosphere generally prevails.

A calmer, more tranquil alternative is the **Alberg Juvenil Palau** (6 C Palau, Tel. 412-5080), which is located in a building from the mid-19th century, close by the Plaça Sant Jaume. It has 40 beds and kitchen facilities for its guests to share. Most rooms have four beds. The doors are closed at midnight.

Apartments. While there are no agencies in Barcelona to facilitate finding an apartment to stay in, there are about 10 different listings in the Generalitat's booklet of hotels, apartments, and camps. They are not in particularly central locations, but are generally comfortable and reasonably priced. The prices begin with rates for one-night stays; longer stays can generally be negotiated at better rates.

Camping. There are a number of camping locations within a 10-mile radius of the city, a number of which are located a few miles to the south along the road that runs between Castelldefels and the airport. The advantage of these is that you are within a few minutes of a long, open, Mediterranean beach. The disadvantage is that you are also under the flight path of jets approaching for a landing at the Prat airport with their accompanying noise. However, in a car Barcelona can be reached in 15 minutes (excluding the odd traffic jam), and there are buses that also run between the city and Castelldefels. The Generalitat rates campgrounds in one of three categories. Among the campsites listed in the top category are:

Cala Godo, at the Centra de la Platja, s/n (Tel. 379-4600). Four miles south of Barcelona toward Castelldefels, it has a capacity for 3,750 people. It is shady and right next to the beach with hot showers, a restaurant, a grocery store, playground for children, and all the amenities you could expect at a campsite. The price is about $15, plus $5 a person ($3 per child), which includes water, electicity, and a hot shower. It's open March 16-Oct. 15, as well as weekends year-round.

La Ballena Alegre ("The Happy Whale"), at kilometer 12.5 on the Castelldefels road driving away from Barcelona (Tel. 658-0504).This is a first-class campground off the road to Castelldefels, with a capacity of 4,300 people. It's open May 15-Sept. 30. Frequently crowded, it's very much a family scene. It has everything a camper needs and is right beside the beach. During the high season, June 21-August 25, prices are $20 plus $5.50 per person ($2.50 per child). During the rest of the year it's somewhat cheaper. The huge sign of a smiling whale makes it hard to miss.

El Toro Bravo, at kilometer 11 of the Castelldefels highway, going toward Castelldefels from Barcelona (Tel. 637-3462). It's open all year, right beside the beach, and offers all the amenities: a bar, restaurant, shopping facilities, hot showers, and tennis courts, with a capacity of 3,600 people. Prices are $5, plus $5 per person ($4 per child), plus another $5 to put up a tent, or $10 for campers.

How to Get Around

Both the metro and bus systems are easy to use and inexpensive and are the recommended mode of travel. Taxis are cheap and plentiful, as well, and many taxi drivers speak at least a little English. For a city that is famous for its nightlife, Barcelona's public transport shuts down surprisingly early. The metros run 5 A.M.-11 P.M., Mon.-Thur.; 6 A.M.-12 P.M. on Sun.; and 5 A.M.-1 A.M. on Fri. and Sat. Buses generally run 6:30 A.M.-10 P.M., although a few, on the busiest routes, also have infrequent night runs. The number to call for general information about public transport—buses, metros, and taxis—is 412-0000. Bus and metro maps are available at the **TMB** office in the **Universitat** metro station on lines 1 and 2, open Mon.-Fri. 8 A.M.-8 P.M.

There is a number to call for information about handicapped access, 412-4444, but you'll need to speak and listen in Spanish. Most of the metro stops built or rebuilt in the past few years do have handicapped access via elevator, but many of the older stations do not.

Also highly recommended as a means of local transport, particularly for sightseeing in the old city, is "shank's mare," i.e., walking. Barcelona is an easy city for walkers. Always pleasant to look at, it is also full of small squares and plazas with a bench or two where you can rest, and if you are thirsty, as well as tired, there is hardly a block in the city that does not offer at least one café with a few outdoor tables. When walking in the city, pay strict attention to the traffic signals for pedestrians at each traffic light. When the signal is green, showing the silhouette of someone walking, you can cross, *in the crosswalk,* and traffic is required to stop for you. This is in theory, and almost every driver in Barcelona obeys that law. However, always be alert crossing streets, and if it appears that a driver may be approaching the crosswalk with no intention of stopping, be prepared to jump out of the way. When the green signal starts to blink, it means you have about three seconds to cross the street, and unless you're fleet it's best not to try and to wait for the signal to go to red and back to green.

TAXIS

Barcelona has some 11,000 black and yellow taxis. They have a green light on their roof medallion which, when lit, means they are free, as well as a sign on the passenger side visor reading *libre,* or *lliure* (Castilian and Catalan), which they also put down when they are available.

Over 1,000 taxis accept credit cards. The driver should be asked at the beginning of the trip if that is how you intend to pay. Prices are quite reasonable and begin at 270 ptas. There is a surcharge for tools, luggage, and animals. Every taxi has a meter. Passengers have the right, by law, to ask for a receipt. Each taxi has an identification number.

Taxis can be hailed in the street, or you can wait at a taxi stand, marked with a *T;* they can also be called on the phone. There are eight companies that you can call by telephone. They are: **Barnataxi** (Tel. 357-7755); **Taxi Radio Movil** (Tel. 358-1111); **Tele Taxi** (Tel. 392-2222); **Radio Taxi Expres** (Tel. 490-2222); **As. Radio Taxi Miramar** (Tel. 433-1020); coop. **Radio Taxi Metropolitana de Barcelona** (Tel. 300-3811); **Taxi Mens** (Tel. 387-1000); and **Ser Taxi** (Tel. 219-9268).

PUBLIC TRANSPORTATION

A T-1 ticket, which can be bought at the ticket booth of any metro station, allows the user 10 rides on either subway or bus and is the best way to go. They cost about 700 pts, or $5.50. There is a machine on the bus into which you insert the T-1 to have the time and date stamped on it. There is also a T-2 ticket, slightly cheaper than the T-1, which can be used only on the metro. Individual fares can be paid when you board a bus and are 125 ptas. While you can board a bus without paying, and tickets are rarely checked, there is a 5,000 ptas. fine for riding without one, and it is safest to obey the law. More than 50 bus routes criss-cross the city, but it is easy enough to figure out which number bus you want by consulting the large map posted at every bus stop, which shows where each bus goes. Bus stops are easily spotted, because they are each marked by a shelter and the picture of a bus mounted on a pole.

The metro offers an alternative to bus transportation, and as subways go it's an excellent one. Each stop, and set of stairs down into the metro, is marked at street level by a large **Metro** sign. The stops are clean, cool, generally safe, and efficient, and there is a large map with clearly marked routes at each station. Individual ride tickets can be bought in each station from vending machines or a manned (or womanned) ticket booth, or you can use your T-1 or T-2 to pass through the turnstiles.

There is also an interurban train line, the **Ferrocarrils de la Generalitat,** which has two lines that run through the city and out to suburban communities. These can be ridden with a T-1 ticket to the outer edge of the city, but you must pay a surcharge if you're going further. For a superb view of the city, ride the ferrocarril to the Av. del Tibadabo, then change to the **tramvia blau** ("blue tram") and take it one stop to the **Peu del Funicular.** This funicular car will carry you up the high hill called Tibidabo to the **Parc d'Attraccions del Tibidabo** ("the Tibidabo Amusement Park"), from where all of Barcelona lies at your feet.

There are other funicular rides as well: one leaves from the metro stop at Parallel on the L-3 line up to the hill called **Montjuïc,** where it connects with the Montjuïc cable car which swings around the Montjuïc amusement park and takes passengers to the castle atop the hill. For more information call 443-0859.

Another funicular ride goes from the **Muelle de los Astilleros** ("Dock of the Shipyards") in the port neighborhood of Barceloneta, across the harbor and up to the foot of Montjuïc. For more information call 442-2270.

AUTO RENTAL

It is not a pleasure to drive in Barcelona. It requires complete concentration, and woe unto the visitor who takes his or her eyes off the traffic for a moment to look at something alongside the street. There are many, many one-way streets in even the most orderly parts of the city, such as the 585-block rectangular grid of streets called the Eixample. Once you begin negotiating the twisting, narrow streets of the old city, things really begin to get hairy.

In short, driving is not particularly recommended. Nevertheless, it does constitute its own kind of adventure, and if it appeals to you there are plenty of places to rent a car. Parking is a continual hassle, unless you are prepared to pay for it in one of the city's parking garages and can find one that has vacant space. Not easy, but not as hard as finding an aboveground spot on the street. In any given neighborhood in Barcelona, it often seems as if more cars are driving around looking for a parking place than are passing through. Another disadvantage to driving is the price of gasoline, which, as in most of Europe, is three to four times higher than the States, although cars are generally smaller and more fuel-efficient.

The following rental car companies have offices at the airport: **Atesa** (Tel. 370-08050); **Avis** (Tel. 478-1706); **Europocar** (Tel. 379-9051); and **Hertz** (Tel. 370-5811).

Among the better-known rental car companies with offices in town are: **Atesa,** 141 C Balmes (Tel. 237-8140); **Avis,** 235 C Aragó (Tel. 487-8754) and 209 C Casanovas (Tel. 209-9533); **Europocar,** 214 C Viladomat (Tel. 439-8403) and 363 C de Consell de Cent (Tel. 488-2398); **Hertz,** 10 C Tuset (Tel. 217-3248); and **Thrifty,** 32 Av. Sarrià (Tel. 430-9071).

BICYCLES

Barcelona is not a particularly bicycle-friendly city, although an increasing effort is being made by the municipal government, the *ajuntament,* to change that.

For instance, there is now a bicycle lane running the length of C de Diputació. There is also one on the tree-lined pedestrian walkway along the upper part of the Av. Diagonal, which continues across the city, alongside the avenue in a somewhat less broad and roomy manner. There are plans to lay out other bicycle-only routes and it may be that in the short-term future things will become much more conducive to bicycling. As it is now, neither pedestrians nor motorized vehicles give much respect to bicyclists. If that's how you intend to get around, don't forget to wear a helmet.

Bikes, including mountain bikes, can be can be rented from a number of places including **Bicitram,** Av. Marquès de l'Argentera, 15 (Tel. 792-2841); **Grup de Treball Bici-Clot,** C Sant Joan de Malta, 1 (Tel. 307-7475); **Passa Two Be,** 81 C Salvador Espiru (Tel. 307-7475); and **Los Filicletos,** Passeig Picasso, 38 (Tel. 319-7885). All of these places rent bicycles by the hour, the half-day, and the whole day.

How to See Barcelona

While riding around on a bus from one beautiful sight to the next listening to a guide may not be the ideal way to see a city, if you're truly limited for time you'll need to do it, just to get an overall sense of the city in a hurry. There are a number of alternatives. One of them, the **Associacó Profesional d'Informadors Turístics de Barcelona** ("Professional Association of Barcelona Tour Guides"), will provide you with a guide and four-hour tour for about $100. Since this rate applies to groups of up to 20 people, groups of four or more people may want to investigate this option.

There are only two main companies offering coach tours of the city: **Julia Tours,** 5 Ronda Universitat (Tel. 317-6454, 317-6209; Fax 318-8494) and **Pulmantur,** 635 Gran Via de les Corts Catalanes (Tel. 317-1297, Fax 318-8497). Both offer tours of about the same duration and itinerary, and both are open year-round. There are four-hour tours in both the morning and afternoon, and they go to about the same places. In the morning (9:30 A.M.-12:30 P.M.) they go to the old city—the barri gòtic—then to the Port Olímpico and the beaches, followed by a drive up Montjuïc to the Olympic Stadium. There are visits to the Cathedral and to the Poble Espanyol at the foot of Montjuïc.

The afternoon tours (3:30 P.M.-6:30 P.M.) travel to the Sagrada Familia and the Passeig de Gràcia and include visits to the Torre de Collserola, that 800-foot-high, insect-like communications tower in the hills designed by the British architect Norman Foster, as well as a stop at Gaudí's Parc Güell and the Museu Picasso.

Each tour costs just shy of $40 per person. There are also full-day tours that touch these spots and include a stop for lunch at the Poble Espanyol for about double that price. These two companies offer nighttime tours as well, with or without dinner included, that feature flamenco music and drinks at a nightclub. Without dinner this one runs about $65; with the food, around $100.

If you want to settle for a little less in terms of a guide's spoken recitation and you are visiting between June 11 and October 12, the best deal in town is the **Bus Turistic,** the number 100 city bus that is just for tourists. Its route covers 15 stops around the city, including many of the most important sites to see in the city. It has an on-board tour guide and printed information about each stop. The ticket also entitles the bearer to discounts at a number of the city's main attractions. A one-day ticket is under $15 and a two-day ticket is below $20, and you buy the ticket when you board the bus. The tour originates in front of the El Corte Inglés department store in the Plaça Catalunya, but you may board anywhere you choose. The ticket allows you to get off and on as many times during the day as you wish, and one comes along every 20 minutes or so from 9 A.M. to 9 P.M. When getting on board, you just show your ticket. The Bus 100 does not run from Oct. 13 to June 10.

For the more romantic, there is still a handful of horse-drawn carts that will take you through town with a coachman to do the driving. To make reservations, call Andres Pujadas at 421-1549; 421-8804. All you have to do is relax and try not to notice the bemused glances of the people you pass. They cost about $25 for a half-hour and will fit four. They only go during daylight hours.

There are two water tours available, and they use a small sightseeing boat called a **golondrina** (swallow). The shorter of the two trips makes a circuit of the port out to the breakwater and takes about 45 minutes. It costs 415 ptas. for adults and 220 ptas. for children under 12 and people over 65. From June 24 to Sept. 27, trips leave from the golondrina mooring, at the port across from the Columbus statue, every 30 minutes daily from 11:30 A.M. to 8 P.M. During the off-season, Sept. 28-June 23, they go from noon to 3 P.M. on weekdays and 11 A.M. to 5:30 P.M. on weekends.

The second trip is a two-hour ride that includes Barceloneta and the Port Olímpic, which costs 1,200 ptas. for adults and 850 ptas. for children under 12 and people over 65. These trips leave three times a day during the summer, from the same mooring, at 11 A.M., 1 P.M., and 4 P.M. On Saturdays, Sundays, and holidays, they leave at 11 A.M., 1 P.M., 4:30 P.M., and 6:30 P.M. During the off-season they leave every day at 11 A.M., 1 P.M., and 4 P.M. (Tel. 442-3106).

Banking and Changing Money

The exchange rate between dollars and **pesetas,** Spain's currency, has fluctuated greatly since the beginning of the 1990s, ranging from a low of about 90 pesetas for every dollar to a high of around 145 per dollar. In the fall of 1996 the rate was about 128 pesetas to the dollar. Travelers will want to check international exchange rates, published in the financial pages of most daily newspapers.

The smallest bill is a 1,000-pta. note. There are also bills in denominations of 2,000 ptas., 5,000 ptas., and 10,000 ptas. Coins come in denominations of 1 pta., 5 ptas. (called a **duro**), 10 ptas., 25 ptas., 50 ptas., 100 ptas., 200 ptas., and 500 ptas.

Most banks will be glad to change foreign currency, and many have a sign in the window in a number of languages, the English part reading: Change. Often the day's exchange rates for major currencies are posted next to this sign. They will charge you a commission, which is not likely to be posted, but which they will be glad to tell you in advance of your transaction if you ask. There are also a number of small currency exchange booths alongside the Rambla. They advertise that they do not charge commissions. This is true, but if you read the small print on their walls you'll see that if you're changing less than $400 they give you a ghastly exchange rate, and it is better to go to a bank and pay the commission. If you're changing a large sum, their exchange rate may come closer to the official bank rate and you might want to inquire at a change kiosk, but do not be too eager to avail yourself of their services until you compare with what a bank will give you.

Banking hours in Barcelona are generally 8:30 A.M.-2 P.M., although many close at 1 P.M. during the height of the summer. In a cash emergency, there are numerous cash machines in bank lobbies, which can be accessed with any credit card around the clock by putting the card in the slot beside the locked outer door. Some of those exchange booths along the Rambla stay open until midnight. Both banks and exchange booths will generally cash traveler's checks.

The American Express office is at 101 Passeig de Gràcia and is open 9:30 A.M.-6 P.M., Mon.-Fri., and 10 A.M.-noon on Saturdays (Tel. 217-0070). There you can exchange traveler's checks without being charged a commission, but the exchange rate is generally lower than what you would get at a bank, so it works out about the same. Generally, if you are cashing under $600 of traveler's checks, it will pay to do so at the American Express office (assuming, of course, that the traveler's checks are American Express). More than that, and you'll probably make out better at a bank.

Credit Cards. American-issued credit cards—Visa, MasterCard, Diner's Club, and American Express—are generally accepted everywhere in Barcelona, with the exception of very small places. Hotels, restaurants, and shops will take them, as will most supermarkets.

Cash Advances. The automated teller machines at banks will usually give cash advances on American-issued Visa cards and MasterCards, provided you enter your personal identification number. Even without that number, bank tellers will do so. Banks charge commissions on both credit card and traveler's check transactions.

Shopping

Now that you've got those pesetas, where are you going to spend them? Not to worry, shopping is a favorite pastime of most Barcelonese, despite prices that generally lift the eyebrows of North Americans. Things like clothes, furniture, and domestic appliances here carry price tags that can reach levels two or three times as high as you would expect to pay in the U.S. Nevertheless, there are the occasional bargains, and many of the shops carry exceptionally lovely, high-quality goods.

The price of everything is subject to an additional **value-added tax,** which at the time of this writing was 16 percent. Non-Spaniards can reclaim that VAT on items for which they pay over 15,000 ptas. and that they bring home with them. July and post-Christmas are the two periods of the year when stores offer sales—**rebaixes** in Catalan, **rebajas** in Castilian. It is against the law to offer cheaper goods at sale prices, and stores are monitored to make sure the goods they offer during these periods are really things they were selling before at higher prices.

Stores are generally open Mon.-Fri., 10 A.M.-2 P.M., then closed for three hours, then open again 5-8 p.m. Some shops are open Saturday mornings, but almost everything closes for Saturday afternoon, and Spanish law requires all stores to close on Sunday except four Sundays before Christmas. Malls built on the stateside model were nonexistent in Barcelona until the past decade, but in the past few years there has been substantial development of mall-type complexes containing numerous shops. Barcelonese seem to enjoy shopping in them and they are growing in popularity. Nevertheless, it is still the small, elegant, family-owned shop that dominates.

Under Franco's dictatorship, the only exception available to buying from local shopkeepers was to visit **El Corte Inglés,** the city's only department store, looming along one side of the Plaça de Catalunya. Eventually, a second Corte Inglés was opened on the edge of the Pedralbes neighborhood on the Av. Diagonal. Even up to the 1990s, the closest thing in Barcelona to a shopping mall was the indoor shopping arcades like the **Bulevard Rosa,** spaces where some 50 or 60 small retail spaces are located. The first of these, and still going strong, is the Bulevard Rosa at 55 Pg. de Gràcia, with shops offering a wide variety of products for sale including clothes, jewelry, perfume, and briefcases.

In 1993, the situation began to change. **L'Illa** opened in time for the Christmas season. It is a shopping mall located off the Av. Diagonal near upscale Pedralbes. The mall features some 130 shops, including a Marks and Spencer, a Disney store, a United Colors of Benetton, a Massimo Dutti menswear store, and a wide array of other nice places, many of them branches of stores known to shoppers across Europe. From in front of the University at the Plaça Universitat buses 63 or 66 will go past it.

There is also a shopping mall in the **Plaça de les Glòries Catalanes** with over 100 stores with a slightly more working-class appeal, as befits the different neighborhood. You can get there on the metro by going to Les Glories on the L-1 red line.

Barcelona has long been known for its textile industry and its leather goods. Lately it's becoming known for its shops featuring high-fashion clothing.

There are a number of outdoor shopping venues worth mentioning. One is **Els Encants,** the flea market, open Mondays, Wednesdays, Fridays, and Saturdays from sun to sun (dawn until dusk). It is also located in the Plaça de les Glòries Catalanes, near the new mall, and can likewise be reached on the L-1 red metro by getting off at the Glòries stop. There is a coin and stamp market—Catalans are avid collectors—in the **Plaça Reial** on Sunday mornings from 9 A.M. to 2:30 P.M. Also on Sundays, there is a used book and magazine market that packs people in elbow-to-elbow around the periphery of the **Mercat de Sant Antoni** ("Saint Anthony's market"), located at the top of the Raval district, from 10 A.M. to 2 P.M. Everything from cheap pornography to classic and rare books is available. Another shopping pleasure is to walk through one of the city's nine covered food markets, any time six mornings a week, and watch people shop for their daily meals.

Barcelona has always been a city of small shops. Catalans have a lot of respect for small businesses, and they like to trade with people they know. Franchises and chain grocery stores, called supermarkets here, have affected local businesses, but people continue to do a lot of their buying from small specialty shops. They prefer waiting in line at the small corner produce shop to buying from the produce department at the local supermarket because they've known the person who runs the small shop all their lives.

Restaurants and Cafés

There are certainly blocks in Barcelona that do not have a restaurant or café, but there seem to be awfully few of them. Studies by the European Union have concluded that Spain has as many bars as all the rest of the EU combined, and Barcelona certainly does its part in contributing to that statistic. In addition, almost all the cafés offer a wide variety of liquid refreshment, supplemented by a few **tapas** (appetizers) displayed in a glass case on the bar, or sandwiches that the bartender will make on request. Many of these cafés have a few tables outside where you can sit during nice weather. In Barcelona's cafés, as all over Europe, once you sit at a table or the bar and order something, that place is yours until you are ready to leave. Stay for 10 minutes or two hours. There are many ways that Barcelonese like to enjoy themselves, but one of the most traditional and enduring is conversation. To meet a friend at a café in the late afternoon and chat for an hour is normal, and one of the great ordinary pleasures of life. Likewise, if you are alone and want to order a coffee and sit reading for an hour, no one is going to bother you.

Coffee in Spain is what we think of as espresso—potent and rich. A **café solo** is a small cup of black coffee served with sugar on the side. A **café con leche** is a large cup with the same amount of coffee and filled with steamed milk. A **cortado** is an espresso with a dash of steamed milk, in a small cup. You can also ask for a **café americano,** which will get you an espresso in a large cup, diluted with water to the approximate strength of an American cup of coffee. Any of the above choices can be made with decaffeinated coffee by simply attaching the word **descafeinado** (des-caf-eh-nahdo) to the end of your order, e.g., *"un café solo descafeinado, por favor."* One of the ways Spaniards like to drink their *café solos* is to add a shot of rum or cognac; this is called a **carajillo de ron,** or a **carajillo de coñac.** The strong coffee and the alcohol make a lovely and energizing synergy together.

Food is a predominant obsession for people all over Spain, and Catalans are no exception. They do not go to a restaurant with the idea of grabbing a bite and leaving. When they sit down to the table, they are there to stay for a while, to work their way leisurely through the courses—which usually consist of, at least, a first course, a second course, dessert, and coffee. A good meal is expected to last a couple of hours at a minimum.

There are numerous restaurants featuring foreign, non-Spanish cuisine in Barcelona, but the visitor with a limited number of meals to eat would be well advised to spend them enjoying the delights of Catalan cooking. As a walk through a Barcelona market will amply illustrate, people here have access to a wide range of ingredients. Seafood is fresh and plentiful, as are vegetables, cheeses, and meats.

For those who want to sample that classic Spanish dish, **paella,** a marvel of saffroned rice, seafood, fish, and whatever else the chef feels like including, there are plenty of places to do so. Paella originated in Valencia and is widely eaten in Barcelona. People regard it as a midday meal, too heavy to eat for supper. The traditional time to eat a paella during the summer is after a couple of hours at the beach, in a restaurant near the water. The truth is that just about anywhere you eat a good paella is fine, as it is one of Barcelona's most toothsome pleasures. Beware, however, of the frozen version called **paelladora** and served in many cafés. It is a pale imitation of the real thing.

Another of the things to take advantage of is the wide variety of olives that are available to buy in the markets, or are served as tapas in bars and cafés. There are olives in all sizes, ranging from tiny to large, and for every taste. There are hot olives, sour olives, sweet olives, olives stuffed with anchovies, olives that have been soaked with garlic and absorbed a hint of its flavor, black olives, green olives—more kinds of olives than you could have imagined existed. A small plate of olives with a glass of cold **fino** (sherry) from Spain's Jerez region in the late afternoon is about as good as it gets.

Barcelona has, of course, a wide variety of restaurants. One thing to keep in mind is that most of them have a daily, fixed-price menu, which will usually include two or three courses, dessert, a drink, and coffee. Ask to see **la menú del dia.**

While Catalan cuisine has a great deal in common with that of the rest of Spain, it has its own delicious dishes, and there are numerous places—from corner cafés to fancy restaurants with white linen tablecloths and sterling silver utensils—to sample it. A person can live a reasonably long lifetime in Barcelona and eat out frequently without exhausting the city's inventory of restaurants and cafés offering tasty food. These places are there for the discovering. Follow your instincts. If a place looks good, even if you can't put your finger on why, stop in and ask to see **la carta.** When you get the menu, look it over, and if the place still looks good, try it. Chances are you'll like it. There's nothing like the pleasure of discovering a good eatery on your own.

Another Catalan specialty is wine. Some of Spain's finest vineyards are in the Penedès region of Catalunya, and the wines that come from here can be of world-class quality. While their taste may equal fine French wines, their prices are usually lower, and many wine lovers find that Barcelona provides them with a wide range of palate pleasers. Also from Penedès is the Catalan version of champagne, called **cava,** the best of which is on a level playing field with fine French champagne. In addition to the wines from Catalunya, there are the fine reds produced in the Rioja region which can almost always be counted on to be decent. White wine from the region of Alella is also well regarded. The way many Barcelonese buy their wine for home consumption is straight out of a cask, mounted on a shelf in a **bodega.** While the traditional bodegas have diminished in number over the years, they are still scattered throughout the city. They are usually dark grottoes with casks lining the wall, each with a different wine at a different price. Folks bring in their own bottles to be refilled.

Spanish beer is quite good, ranging from the relatively mild **San Miguel** to the stronger **Voll Damm Extra.** There is a dark beer called **Bock Damm,** which is quite tasty. When asking for a draft beer in a bar, ask for a **caña** (pronounced canya). A small bottle of beer is a **quinto** and a regular-sized bottle is a **mediana.** Water is not automatically brought to the table as in the States; you must buy bottled water, **con gaz** (carbonated) or **sin gaz** (uncarbonated). A sample menu, with dishes in both Catalan and Castilian, is included in the back of this book. When ordering, it is the norm to ask for both your first and second course at the same time.

Among the most basic Catalan dishes, available in many places, are **espinacs a la catalana,** spinach sauteed with pine nuts and raisins, and **mongetes amb butifarra,** white beans and the tasty butifarra sausage. There are also some seasonal tastes available. Winter is marked by the appearance on many corners of small huts where chestnuts and sweet potatoes are roasted on charcoal braziers.

Late winter is the season for **calçots,** an oversized green onion only available at this time of year. These are grilled until charred on their thin outside skins. Then they are brought to the table, six or eight to a plate, along with a special kind of thick sauce called **romescu,** made from tomatoes, almonds, and garlic. The calçot is dipped in the sauce and stuffed into the mouth, messy and delicious. Restaurants provide a bib for diners to wear while they eat them. They are only available in February and March, and everyone has their favorite restaurant for eating calçots while they last.

One sure sign that spring has arrived in Barcelona is when the **horchaterias** open their doors, and **horchata** appears on café menus all over town. An horchata is a cold, sweet, thin beverage, like a watery almond milkshake, which originated in Valencia and is made from the root of a bush called *chufa* (pronounced choofa). It is something of an acquired taste, but should be sampled in a café just for the experience. It is also sold in liters for people to take home.

While each individual will have his or her favorite places to eat in Barcelona, there are numerous time-tested recommendations included in this book. An inexpensive meal, with wine, will cost under $25 per person, a medium-priced meal between $25 and 50, and an evening at an expensive restaurant, over $50. You may have some trouble paying with a credit card at the corner café, but not in other places. The places discussed in this book accept major credit cards unless otherwise stated. *Bon profit* ("enjoy your meal"), as the Catalans say.

Living It Up

Barcelona is known across Europe for its nightlife. There are a wide variety of clubs, including scores of "designer" bars, created by some of the city's finest designers. A great deal of creativity has been employed in these places, and many of them are worth a look-see, even if you don't want to stay and revel. North Americans over the age of 30 have a hard time appreciating the city's nightlife, because it does not really get rolling until 1 A.M., an hour when many an older American is already running out of steam. There are many clubs that do not close their doors until 5 or 6 A.M. on weekends, and some that go until well into the morning.

Drunks are relatively scarce in Barcelona, but drink is not. People rarely drink to excess here, but they frequently drink. Bars are everywhere, and they range in kind from the worker's watering hole on the corner to discrete, elegant cocktail bars where you can sit on plush furniture and sip your drink.

For those who have the youthful energy that is required in a town where the discotheques do not begin to fill up until after midnight, a number of them have been included herein. Many of these places have cover charges; it is not cheap to spend an evening drinking and dancing in Barcelona. The city has its share of jazz clubs, the best of which I have also included.

As jazz is often called a truly American music, so it could be said that flamenco is a truly Spanish music, filtered through the strength of its gypsies as jazz has been filtered through the trajectory of African-Americans. But because flamenco is more closely associated with Andalucia than with Catalunya, it has fewer fans in Barcelona than elsewhere in the country.

Most of the flamenco performed on a regular basis here has traditionally been for tourists. However, don't let this scare you away, because for someone who has never experienced the power of flamenco singing and guitar playing, these shows can be eye-openers. While they do not feature the best flamenco, the clubs listed in this book do generally offer professionals of decent quality. In addition, in what is probably a cyclical swing in cultural tastes, flamenco is becoming appreciated to a growing extent by the younger generation of Catalans, who are realizing that it is an extraordinarily soulful music. To find out who is playing at the live music venues, consult the **Cartelera** in the daily newspapers. Also included in this book are a number of places where the older, more subdued set can go for a quiet cocktail in a dimly-lit ambience with comfortable seating and a noise level that does not preclude conversation.

Cinema. Barcelona is very much a moviegoer's city. There are always a number of films showing in their original language with subtitles in Castilian. Films are listed every day in the Cartelera section of the daily papers, and a film listed with *v.o.* in parentheses means "version original." The multi-cinema, called the **Verdi,** in the Gràcia neighborhood (32 C Verdi, Tel. 327-0562), has five screens. A sister cinema on the block behind it has four, all showing films from around the world in their original versions, with Spanish subtitles. These films are often in English. There are a number of other cinemas around the city that show v.o. films, including the **Casablanca** (115 Pg. de Gràcia, Tel. 218-4345); the six-screen **Renoir Les Corts** (12 Eugeni d'Ors, Tel. 490-5510); and the **Arkadin** (103 Travessera de Gràcia, Tel. 405-2222). In addition, a 15-screen complex, Barcelona's largest, named the **Icària-Yelmo,** opened in the summer of 1996 in the Port Olimpic (Tel. 221-7585). All 15 screens show v.o., although this policy engendered quite a few skeptics, who predicted that it would be short-lived. Cinemas have a "day of the spectator" one day during the week when tickets are sold at a reduced price, on either a Monday or Wednesday, depending on the cinema. This, too, is listed in the Cartelera. By the end of 1996 there were over 20 screens that regularly showed films in English, but despite the growth in their numbers, the growth in their popularity has been even more rapid. If you go to the Verdi or the Renoir or the Casablanca on a weekend night, get there early to avoid standing in long lines.

Classical Music. This is best heard at the **Palau de la Música Catalana,** not for the acoustics, which are only fair to middling, but for the hall itself, which is one of the great Modernist creations and an incredible fantasy of a theater. There is also opera at the **Liceu,** the extraordinary opera house that burned to the ground in 1993 but promises to reopen for its 150th anniversary in 1997. This was an opera house in the grand tradition before it burned, and one hopes it will be so reconstructed. Events at these places and other classical concerts around the city are also listed in the Carteleras of *La Vanguardia* or *El País*. Tickets can be purchased in advance at the theaters.

There are fairly frequent recitals in the city's various churches—usually free—and a medieval cathedral can be a marvelous place to hear music. These, too, are usually listed in the Cartelera.

Dance. This is, lamentably, a city without much in the way of permanent dance venues. The only classical ballet is generally afforded by touring groups based in other places. Some of the local modern dance companies have international reputations, but no space to call home in their own city. Companies move around from one venue to another. The **Mercat de Flors** ("Flower Market") has been converted into a lovely and comfortable performance space, and dance pops up at small theatres all over town, but there is not anywhere stable. For information about specific dance companies working when you arrive, check the Cartelera in a daily newspaper or go by the **Associació dals Professionals de Danza de Catalunya** ("the Professional Dance Association of Catalunya") at 52 Via Laietana (Tel. 416-0068). You may or may not find someone there who speaks English.

Electricity, Temperature, and Time

Like most of Europe, Barcelona operates on the metric system, degrees Celsius, 220 volts, and a television and video system incompatible with that of North America.

If you bring anything electrical, it should have an adapter switch for 220 volts, and you'll need to also have a plug adapter with prongs that push into the sockets. However, there is no need to worry about battery-operated appliances, because the batteries you buy in Barcelona work fine in anything, and are widely available.

A good formula for converting temperatures in Celsius into Fahrenheit is the following: Multiply degrees Celsius by two, subtract 10 percent, and add 32. For instance, if it's 22 degrees Celsius, multiply by two—44—subtract 10 percent—40—and add 32—and *voila,* 72 degrees Fahrenheit.

Spaniards use the 24-hour clock to express time—what North Americans call military time. If something is open from 16:00 to 20:00, that means 4-8 P.M. A concert that starts at 22:30, as many do, will begin at 10:30 P.M.

Spain (except for the Canary Islands where it is an hour earlier) is six hours ahead of the eastern time zone in the U.S. That means if it is 4 P.M. in Barcelona, it is 10 A.M. in New York; 9 A.M. in New Orleans; 8 A.M. in Denver; and 7 A.M. in Los Angeles. Spain goes on daylight saving time at the end of March and returns to regular time at the end of September, almost a month sooner than in the United States.

Health

Air pollution is not a major problem in Barcelona at the level it is in, say, Los Angeles or Mexico City, but there is lots of traffic in a small space and there are days when the air is heavy. Air quality varies from day to day, but it is rarely worse than most big cities. Hay fever sufferers may be troubled and should bring their medications. At the height of the summer, when the thermometer rises above 33 degrees Celsius, it is wise to avoid going out in the midday sun. A heavy Barcelona lunch with wine, followed by a trip to the beach and a couple of hours under the sun, is not advised. Exercise caution and common sense when the weather is hot.

Swimming at the beaches is generally safe, unless there is a red flag prominently displayed indicating that the beach has been closed to swimmers, or a yellow flag indicating caution.

Water from the taps can be drunk with no ill effects to health thanks to a large dose of chlorine, which makes it taste rather unpleasant. The majority of Barcelonese drink bottled water, and you will want to do the same. However, if you are on the street and are thirsty, and you pass one of the many working water fountains in the city, all the authorities say you can drink from it with no trouble other than a fairly high level of chlorine and a moderately unpleasant flavor.

Barcelona, and Catalunya as a whole, has among the highest numbers of HIV+ residents of any autonomous region in Spain. The sale of condoms was illegal until after Franco died, and their use here is still lower than it should be. Condoms are sold in pharmacies, where they are not usually displayed, although the pharmacist will be glad to let you choose from a limited assortment. This is changing as more and more pharmacies do display condoms and try to make it easier for customers to buy them. Currently, the larger supermarkets may also offer them in their toiletries sections. There have been numerous publicity campaigns encouraging people to practice safe sex. How effective they have been is not absolutely clear. Visitors, at any rate, should be aware that AIDS is here and safe sex should be the absolute rule.

For those who think of tobacco as a health issue, Barcelona is not a pleasant city. Smoking is still a national vice in Spain, and there are no non-smoking sections in public places. Furthermore, no one feels hesitant about smoking in another person's home, around their children, or anywhere else. It is a generally held notion here that smoking has been entirely banned in the United States, and Spaniards resist any suggestion of following the example of the U.S. in treating smoking as a social ill to be addressed with prohibition. Those who enjoy a good cigar should be aware that the tobacco stores offer a wide range of Cuban imports ranging from

Partagas to Montecristos to Cohibas. They are expensive, but since they're unobtainable in the States, you might want to indulge. The Spanish word for cigar is *puro*. Many Spanish men are enthusiastic cigar smokers, and almost every restaurant and café keeps a humidor on hand, full of a range of cigars. If you want one after a meal, simply ask for a puro and make your selection when the humidor is brought to the table.

Well-being—if not health itself—in a strange city often depends on being able to find a toilet when one is far from a hotel room and reluctant to stop long enough to purchase the rights to one by having something in a café. The best bet are the pay toilets scattered around town. They are big green portable potties, marked *WC*, which take 25 ptas. to admit you inside. These are fairly plentiful, usually clean, and okay. In addition, a recent survey carried out by a male and female reporter from a local newspaper found that when they went into a bar or café and asked to use the toilet, they were almost always granted permission. When in a bar, the proper way to ask for directions to the restroom is to ask, *"Donde estan los servicios?"*

Sports

There are several golf courses and driving ranges around Barcelona, all within 15 miles of the city. Reservations are needed at any of the golf courses. The **Club de Golf El Prat** (Tel. 379-0278), near the airport, is regarded as the city's best course. There are also the **Club de Golf San Cugat** (Tel. 674-3908); the **Club de Golf Terramar,** Sitges (Tel. 894-0580); and the **Club de Golf Vallromanes** (Tel. 572-9064). Golf is not thought of as a sport open to the general public. Equipment is much more expensive than in England or the U.S. and greens fees are astronomical by North American standards, often between $50 and $100 for eighteen holes.

Joggers can use the track at the **Ciutadella Park.** The road up to Montjuïc is also a favorite of joggers who like a steep uphill run, and once at the top of the hill there are several jogging trails. For something a little more rural there are the paths that wind through the wooded hills above the city, **La Collserola.**

Swimmers have a wide choice of locales in which to practice their sport. Apart from the many miles of beaches within easy reach, there are some two dozen public pools around the city. Most charge small fees and are open at varying hours. A complete list can be obtained at a tourist office.

Tennis players can also tread the same ground used in the 1992 Olympics by playing at the **Centre Municipal de Tenis del Vall d'Hebron,** 178 Passeig Vall d'Hebron (Tel. 427-6500). Reservations are necessary here and at all tennis courts. There are no free courts in Barcelona. An hour of tennis will cost between 750 and 1,800 ptas., depending on the condition of the courts and the locker rooms. The Vall d'Hebron courts range from 1,500 to 2,000 ptas. per hour. Just on the other side of the airport is the seaside town of Castelldefels. There are a number of tennis clubs here that rent courts to non-members, such as the **Sports Catalunya,** just across the road from the Canal Olimpic, where some of the Olympic rowing competition was held in 1992. It has eight courts for rent at 800 ptas. an hour, which includes locker room facilities with showers; you should reserve ahead of time. It's just off the Autovia Castelldefels ("Castelldefels highway") at Kilometer 17.3 (Tel. 636-0011). It's fun to play here, then cross the autovia and carry on a couple of blocks to the beach where you can have a swim. Also just outside the other end of the city is the **Club Canmalich,** Av. 11 de Setembre (Tel. 372-8211), in the town of Sant Just Desvern.

There is plenty of fishing in and around Barcelona. First and foremost is surfcasting from jetties and beaches that can be reached by metro or bus. There is also trout fishing in the streams up north, and a handful of large lakes all within two hours of the city. **Riper** is the best fishing store in the city. They have all kinds of equipment as well as live and artificial bait. They are at 12 C de Tallers (Tel. 302-6981), two long blocks away from the corner of C de Tallers and the Rambla.

You need a license to fish in fresh water and another to fish in the sea. They run about $12 apiece and can be obtained from the Generalitat's department of woods and wildlife by going by the office with the fee and a photocopy of your passport. The office is open 9 A.M.-2 P.M. and 3:30-5:30 P.M., Mon.-Fri., and is located about a block below the Av. Diagonal behind the Princess Sofia Hotel at 22-24 C Sabino de Arana (Tel. 330-6451).

Skiers can consult a Spanish tourist office before they come, or go to the **tourist office** in the Plaça de Catalunya (Tel. 304-3134) and request information on ski slopes in Catalunya. Any travel agent in Barcelona during the winter will be able to offer you a package deal to the Pyrenees with bus transportation, hotel, meals, and lift tickets included. These range considerably in terms of quality in both accomodations and slopes, so try to be as specific as possible when describing what you want to the travel agent. A number of ski resorts also offer cross-country trails.

For those who prefer to enjoy their sports as spectators rather than participants, there are also some options. While many think of bullfighting when they think of Spain, Catalans are notoriously indifferent to the **corrida.** There is, however, one huge, impressive, bullfighting arena, patronized mostly by tourists and Spaniards who have come from other parts of the country to live here. It is the **Plaça de Toros Monumental,** 743 Gran Via de les Corts Catalanes (Tel. 453-3821), where fights are held every Sunday at 5:30 P.M. in April, May, and from Aug. 15 to Sept. 31. In June and July they begin at 6 P.M. Advance tickets are available at the corner of C Aribau and Gran Via.

The great spectator sport in Barcelona is soccer. The **Fútbol Club (F.C.) Barcelona,** known as el Barça, is a world-class soccer team and is the reigning passion of Barcelonese. The home stadium, **Estadi Camp Nou** (not far from the Hotel Princess Sofia and the outer reaches of the Av. Diagonal, at 12-18 Av. Arístides Maillol, Tel. 330-9411), holds over 120,000 and is often sold out during the season, particularly when arch-rival Real Madrid comes to town. There are two seasons each year, occupying the fall and the spring. If you like soccer, an el Barça match is something you won't soon forget. This is the best and perhaps the only way to understand the city's relationship to soccer and to the club. It's not cheap. A seat will cost you at least $35, and then you'll be sitting pretty high up in a stadium that holds 120,000 people. The more expensive seats go for over $100 apiece for any league match. Still, for soccer lovers, it's worth the expense. This is where you'll find the complete ardor and devoted fans that many mistakenly associate with bullfighting before they come to Barcelona. Camp Nou is where Catalan fans let it all hang out.

There is a second major-league Barcelona soccer team, **El Espanyol,** which has its own stadium, **Sarría,** at 2-4 Ricardo Villa (Tel. 203-4800). The stadium is much smaller than Camp Nou, holding only 42,000 people, but it is still a fun place to watch a match—although no cheaper. The team has a smaller but no less devoted following among Barcelonese.

Telephones and Post Office

There are public telephones, with operators (such a place is called a **locutorio telefonicó**) who will place long-distance calls, in the main vestibule of the train station at **Sants,** open daily from 8 A.M. to 10:45 P.M., which also has fax service; the bus station at **Barcelona Nord,** open Mon.-Fri., 8 A.M.-9 P.M. (Tel. 265-7094); and at **La Rambla,** 88 (Tel. 412-7026), open daily from 10 A.M. to 11 P.M., also with fax service. Pay phones require a minimum of 20 ptas. to function, but you might as well begin with a 25-pta. coin. Insert your money, then dial your number. The amount of money remaining is displayed on the phone, and when you get down close to zero it's best to add more to keep from being suddenly cut off. Telephone cards are also available at tabacs.

When calling from other parts of Spain, or within Europe, the area code for Barcelona is 93, followed by the local number. When calling from the States, the country code is 34 and the city code is 3, followed by the local number.

Stamps are available at any **tabac,** i.e., where they sell tobacco products. These places have a big *T* prominently displayed outside. The person working in the tabac will weigh a letter or package for you and sell you the appropriate postage.

Public mail boxes are painted yellow and are numerous. Local mail goes in the slot on the left as you face it, and mail for anywhere outside Barcelona goes in the slot on the right, marked *Provincias y extranjero*. Postcards and letters require the same amount of postage.

If you want to receive mail and don't know which hotel you'll be in, or how long you'll be there, the best bet is to have your mail sent to you at **Lista de Correos,** Pl. Antoni Lopez, 1, 08002 Barcelona. This is the main post office and is located a few blocks north of the Ramblas, across from the waterfront.

The telephone number for the post office is 318-3831, although to find out if you have mail you must go there and stand in line at the Poste Restante windows, numbers 34-36, on the main floor. Take your passport, because without it you won't get your mail. Open 8 A.M.-10P.M., Mon.-Fri.; 9 A.M.-8 P.M. Saturday; and 9 A.M.-1 P.M. Sunday.

Packages can be sent from most post offices, which are marked by a yellow sign that says **Correo.** Mail can be sent air mail or surface. Surface is cheaper, but will take from two to four months to arrive in the U.S., while air mail usually takes a week to 10 days. If you are particularly concerned that something arrive, pay a little extra to send it *certificado*. You fill out a small form saying where it is going and who's sending it. The package gets stamped certificado, and you keep your copy of the form so the package or letter can be traced if it doesn't arrive. You can also pay a little more and send it *urgente*. Such a letter will arrive at its U.S. destination in about four days.

Television and Radio

During the first half of the 1990s, Barcelona had essentially six free television networks and one subscription cable network. Two of the channels—**TVE1** and **TVE2**—are national, public stations, although both air some commercials. There is also **TV-3,** a Catalan language station, and **TV-33,** a second Catalan channel. These also carry ads. There are two private, national networks, **Antenna 3** and **Tele 5,** which have much more frequent commercial interruptions, and one cable network, **Canal+,** which carries no ads except for its own programming, and costs about $20 a month. While most of the programming on Canal+ is scrambled for those who don't subscribe, one thing that is not scrambled is the previous day's "ABC Evening News" from the States, which airs on Canal+ at 7 A.M. Monday-Friday.

Those with a satellite dish can, of course, receive any number of programs in a variety of languages. At the end of 1995, a law was passed to permit and introduce cable television and outline the way in which cable contracts would be awarded. Despite having a limited number of channels, Spaniards already were watching more daily hours of television per capita than any other Europeans, so the cable market obviously represents lucrative profit potential, and cable is expected to be widely available by the end of 1997. The channel configuration that will result is anyone's guess. The Popular Party, which began to govern in 1996, is determined to stop the flow of red ink at the public networks—TV1 and TV2—and it is possible they will be merged and pared down. Whatever the number of channels available when you visit, the day's programming can be found in the daily newspapers. *El País, El Periódico,* and *La Vanguardia* are the three daily newspapers in Castilian and each carries complete television listings.

During the summer of 1996, a free monthly magazine in English, the *Barcelona Metropolitan,* appeared. While it is aimed primarily at English-speaking residents of the city, it is also a valuable aid to those who want to understand Barcelona. It is a good guide to what is going on, as it lists films in v.o. and art exhibits. It is distributed in numerous cinemas, bars, hotels, bookstores, and consulates.

Magazines in general are much appreciated here, as a browse through any newsstand will show. Particularly loved are the weekly magazines like *Hola* that chronicle the lives and loves of Spain's rich and famous. Foreign press is available in a number of stores along the Pg. de Gràcia, as well as at the newsstands all along the Rambla.

Visitors from the U.S. need to remember that the tower of Babel is alive and well in videoland, and that videotape recorded on European equipment cannot be viewed on Stateside equipment, and recorded tapes brought from home will not be watchable on European equipment. Your U.S.-bought video camera can use blank tape bought in Europe to record on, but you will not be able to see the results until you get home, because your camera is recording for American equipment.

Radio is popular in Barcelona and there are numerous stations, both public and private, and in both the city's official languages. English-language radio is nonexistent, but English songs, particularly pop and rock and roll, are frequently heard.

English-Language Books and Newspapers

For daily news from the States there are basically two choices: the *International Herald Tribune* (published jointly by the *Washington Post* and the *New York Times*) and *USA Today*'s international edition. These are available at any of the news kiosks along the Rambla, and in many other kiosks around the old city. There are a number of bookstores that carry English-language books, some of them with a wide, interesting selection, and others with only a shelf or two of paperback thrillers and mysteries. There is also a good, secondhand bookshop called **Bookstore,** in an out-of-the-way location far above Diagonal at 13 C La Granja, about three blocks from the metro stop Lesseps on the green line (L-3). Trade in your old books, and they'll drastically reduce their already cheap prices.

There are two English-language libraries. One is at the **British Council** (C Amigo, 38, Tel. 209-1364) and the other is at the **Institute of North American Studies** (Via Augusta, 123, Tel. 200-7551). Both are open to the public. At the first one, you can read British reference books, newspapers, and periodicals, and at the other the same selection is available from the States. The British Council stopped lending books at the end of 1996, after 50 years. The North American Institute's collection is good, the chairs are comfortable, and the staff is friendly and helpful. Checkout privileges are available for 3,500 ptas a year. Unfortunately, there are no metro stops nearby on the Via Augusta. You can take a 64 or 58 bus from the Plaça de la Universitat, which goes up C Aribau and will drop you at Aribau-Via Augusta, from which you can walk a couple of blocks to the institute.

Religion

Catholicism was the state religion in Spain under Franco. These days, religious tolerance is the law. While the great majority of religious Spaniards are Catholics, numerous other religions are represented in Barcelona. There is one kosher butcher for observant Jews and a number of halal butchers for observant Muslims. Among the various religious centers here are the following:

Catholic Mass in English: Sundays, 10 A.M., Parroquia Maria Reina, Ctra. d'Espluges, 103, Tel. 203-5539
Anglican Mass in English: Saint George Church, C Sant Joan de la Salle, 41, Tel. 418-6978
Seventh Day Adventists, 133 C Comte d'Urgell, Tel. 453-3136
Evangelical Church, 167 Av. del Paral.lel, Tel. 325-1667
Methodist and Presbyterian Esglèsia Evangèlica, 51 C Arago, Tel. 228-7712
Buddhist, Centre de Budisme Social de Barcelona, 39 C Aribau, Tel. 451-1922
Jehovah's Witnesses, 21 C Pintor Fortuny, Tel. 318-0909
Mormon Community, 37 C Marquès de Sentmenat, Tel. 321-5525
Jewish Community Synagogue, 24 C Avenir, Tel. 200-6148
Islamic Centre Mosque, 326 Av. Meridiana, Tel. 351-4901
Toarek Ben Ziad Mosque, 91 C de la Hospital, Tel. 441-9149

Museums

Unless otherwise noted, the museums have an admission charge (usually between $3 and $7). For the smaller, more specialized museums, a call ahead to check the hours they are open is recommended.

Emergency Services

The best thing to do in a medical emergency is to call the **Barcelona Medical Centre,** which is open 24 hours a day to provide medical assistance and referrals to foreigners. The telephone number is 290-6859.

You can also call the **U.S. Consulate,** which is located at 23 Pg. Reina Elisenda in the upscale, fairly inaccessible district of Pedralbes. It is open Mon.-Fri., 9 A.M.-5 P.M., and the phone is 280-2227. The consulate also has an emergency number for reaching the duty officer at any time through an answering service. That number is 414-1100, and if you call and leave your phone number, someone should get back to you within half an hour.

Pharmacies in Barcelona take turns staying open around the clock, and a listing of those nearest a given location is posted beside the door of closed pharmacies.

Should you need to report a crime, the Barcelona police maintain a station to help foreigners. It is located at 43 La Rambla, only a few blocks up from the port. If you are not near here and need help, or are the victim of a crime, stop any uniformed police officer. The emergency number to dial for assistance on the telephone is 061, although it's doubtful you'll find someone on the other end who can speak English.

Of course, if you have an emergency while you are in a hotel, the best place to go for help is the front desk.

Learning the Languages

Catalan. There are numerous places sponsored by the government of Catalunya that offer a range of courses from beginning to advanced. The price is usually low, and occasionally free. The university also offers intensive courses at higher prices. For more information call the **Centre de Normalització Lingüística de Barcelona** at 162 C de Pau Claris (Tel. 482-0200). Open 9 A.M.-2 P.M., 3-5:30 P.M., Mon.-Fri. For university courses, it's the **Servei de Llengua Catalana** (Tel. 318-4266).

Spanish. Per semester, the best price/quality ratio is at the **Escola Oficial d'Idiomes** (Tel. 329-2458), which offers courses at a number of levels, taught by professionals for around $100 for three months of classes, two hours every weekday. However, enrollment is usually tight and aspiring new students participate in a drawing for the allotment of places. It's at the end of Av. Drassanes near the port and doesn't have a street number. It's open 10:30 A.M.-12:30 P.M. and 4:30-5:30 P.M. Mon.-Fri. for those seeking information.

The **International House** (Tel. 268-4511) offers intensive Spanish courses at all levels. It's at 14 C Trafalgar and is open from 8 A.M.-9 P.M., Mon.-Fri.

The **Universitat de Barcelona** (Tel. 318-4266) offers courses throughout the year in its Estudios Híspanicos department. These are geared toward foreigners at a range of levels from beginning conversation to advanced courses in Spanish literature. The university is at 585 Gran Via de les Corts Catalanes at the Plaça Universitat and the office for language course information is open from 9 A.M.-1 P.M., Mon.-Fri.

Lost and Found

This office is located at 9 C de la Ciutat, around the corner from the Ajuntament and the Plaça Sant Jaume (Tel. 402-3161). You can't count on finding someone there who speaks English, so be prepared. They are open Mon.-Fri., 8:30 A.M.-2:30 P.M.

2

Getting to Know Barcelona

Getting Your Bearings

Barcelona is a city of neighborhoods, *barris* (in Catalan) or *barrios* (in Castilian), and this book approaches it as such. The metropolitan area has developed over the course of 2,000 years, slowly expanding outwards and incorporating, one after another, the individual villages that had sprung up at the city's edges. For those whose time in Barcelona is limited to a day or two, there is enough in the old city to keep them fully occupied and happy. But for those with a little more time to spend, or the stamina to pack more into a limited stay, excursions into less well-known parts of the city will pay off handsomely.

Make a list of what you want to see and allow plenty of time to get around. For those whose time is extremely limited, an arbitrary ranking of the city's top 10 must-see sights is included below, as well as a suggested general itinerary for a four-day visit. In addition to allowing time to get from one place to the next (bearing in mind that the trip between two spots can often turn up the most interesting facets of your own Barcelona experience), be sure to give yourself time for the morning, afternoon, and evening stops in bars and cafés along the way for a little something, enjoying the same pauses to refresh that punctuate the day for Barcelona's residents and that visitors, too, will find to be a help in maintaining stamina and appreciating the city's vibrant café life.

Barcelonese orient themselves by up and down, up being away from the port and the Mediterranean, down being closer to it. Thus they will give you an address and tell you it's on the right hand going up, i.e., heading away from the water. For foreigners, the heart of the city—and the point from which it is easiest to orient oneself—is the top of La Rambla, across the street from the Plaça de Catalunya. From here you can walk up toward the sleek districts of the Eixample or down toward the port and digress into either part of the old city: the barri gòtic on your left going down, or the Raval and barrio chino on your right. Likewise, the metro station at the Plaça de Catalunya is a major interchange of metro lines, and there is also a Ferrocaril (commuter train) stop there.

Barcelona's Top 10 Sights

There are many, many things to see and do in Barcelona, and a person's favorites are necessarily heavily weighted toward their tastes. However, the following 10 items are usually pretty high on everyone's list and will provide you with a starting point to begin thinking about what is out there.

1. La Rambla. As mentioned above, this is pretty much the heart of the city. A stroll down any part of its length will give you an idea of the diversity and charm of the city. Sooner or later, and with some regularity, almost all of Barcelona's residents find themselves on the Rambla for some reason.

2. La Sagrada Familia. Antoni Gaudí's unfinished phantasm of a cathedral is among those one-of-a-kind buildings on the globe. There is nothing else like it.

3. La Mansana de la Discòrdia ("The Block of Discord"). This block of three modernist buildings on the Passeig de Gràcia done by Gaudí, Domenech i Mutaner, and Puig i Cadalfach, is, perhaps, the most remarkable street in a city full of amazing architecture.

4. Roman Barcelona and the Museu d' Història de la Ciutat. Follow in the footsteps of the Romans, walking the streets they did. There are 16 points along the length of this two-hour walk, mapped out in a free brochure from the Museu d'Història de la Ciutat, where you can journey back to Roman times.

5. Museu d'Art Contemporani. This great white whale of a museum, built by American architect Richard Meiers, opened in 1995 and has an interior architecture to match its extraordinary exterior.

6. Montjuïc. The Miro Foundation is on this high hill, as are the Olympic Stadium and a series of marvelous vistas of the city below spreading out to the sea.

7. Port Olímpic. This is Barcelona-by-the-sea with beaches, cafés, and a pier with excellent restaurants where you can dine while looking out across the water.

8. Museu Picasso. Early Picasso, including some excellent works from the artist's pre-cubist days, which he left to the museum's foundation.

9. Palau de la Música Catalana. If it's not the only modernist concert hall in the world, it is surely the most amazing.

10. Surrounding Catalunya. Take your choice—the breathtaking sheer stone summits of Montserrat or the surrealism of the Salvador Dalí museum in Figueres.

Barcelona in One to Four Days

Even those who are only going to be a short time in Barcelona should try to appreciate life *à la Catalana* and adapt to long lunches and late dinners. Despite the frenetic nightclub life of the young, and the late hours of older adults, this is a part of the world with a slower pace of life than in Anglo-Saxon countries or Japan, where sitting outside having a relaxed conversation and a cup of something is as much a part of life as any of the sights you may be seeing. Conserve some energy during the day so you can get a taste of Barcelona by night, whatever your tastes in evening activities may be.

Day 1: Take a three-hour guided tour and spend the other part of the day walking down the Rambla, exploring the barri gòtic, and just ambling where your feet may take you.

Day 2: Buy a ticket on a Bus 100 and take the time to get off and explore those things the guided tour whetted your appetite to explore further.

Day 3: Visit the Church of Santa María del Mar and the Picasso Museum, which are within a few blocks of one another, have a seafood lunch in Barceloneta, and explore the Olympic Port.

Day 4: Visit the Museu d'Art Contemporani ("Contemporary Art Museum") and the Raval district in the morning. In the afternoon, visit the Parc Ciutadella with its lovely fountains, its zoo, and the small Museum of Modern Art, which features art that is not so modern at all, but is by turn-of-the-century Catalan painters, some of whom were excellent.

La Ciutat Vella

La Ciutat Vella, the old city, basically consists of two parts: the **barri gòtic** ("gothic neighborhood"), built in the Middle Ages in the same general neighborhood where the Romans had their city, and the **Raval** district, which dates back to the mid-18th century. Dividing these two parts of the old city is one of the world's great pedestrian boulevards, the **Rambla,** a wide, mile-long strip that runs down from the Plaça de Catalunya to the statue of Christopher Columbus at the port.

The medieval neighborhood, the barri gòtic, is not a pristine preserve set aside to be admired in a museum-like stasis. To the contrary, it is teeming with life. Laundry hangs from balconies; people pass by with the fruits of their daily errands in their hands—a loaf of fresh bread wrapped in paper, a string bag full of the cheese, olives, meat, and vegetables that will be today's midday meal—and shopkeepers stand in their doorways chatting with neighbors.

Part of the pleasure of wandering these streets consists in losing oneself, and losing the preconceived notions of cities we bring with us, particularly those of us from the New World. Barcelona's old city is a place where people have lived together in a beautiful urban setting by the sea for over a thousand years, and just wandering through it with our eyes open is a treat. It is the unexpected sights of life in progress here—rounding a corner in a narrow cobblestone street and seeing two old men in berets leaning on canes and chatting in the twilight—that often remain as the most pleasant memories long after a trip is over and the photos have been put away.

These memories you will have the joy of gathering for yourself. I cannot direct you to them, but what I can do is suggest, after years of losing myself in the streets of the old city, a couple of exceptionally pleasant routes to use as the norms from which you should by all means deviate according to the whim of the moment.

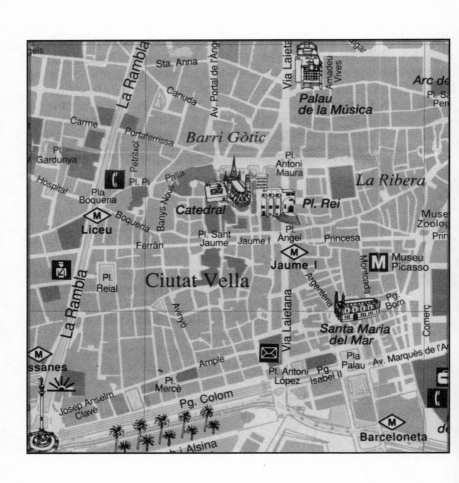

3

The Rambla

1. Orientation

Probably the best single walk in Barcelona is simply to walk the length of the Rambla, from the Plaça de Catalunya down to the sea. This is the backbone of the old city, to which everything connects in some way. During the Middle Ages, the Rambla marked the southern frontier of the walled city. The word comes from the Arabic *rambla,* meaning a watercourse, and is thought to refer to the waste stream that was just outside the city walls.

Over the centuries, it was filled in with rocks, waste, and garbage, and during the Middle Ages a number of churches and convents were built beside it, serving as a place for city and country to come together. On the rural side of these ecclesiastical buildings was open countryside, where farmers worked the soil. It was at this place just outside the walls where markets sprang up alongside the churches and convents. Originally, these were probably nothing more than places where farmers came to stand and sell a few vegetables or a basket of fruit. Gradually, the market began to get more organized, and it is on this site where Barcelona's largest food market, **La Boqueria,** is presently located.

The Rambla began to take on its present shape between 1770 and 1860, when the wall came down and the Rambla was filled in and turned into a boulevard. At the same time, the countryside to the south became gradually citified, and evolved as the Raval district.

Today's Rambla is actually composed of four different sections, and for this it is sometimes referred to in the plural as Las Ramblas. Beginning at the top by the Plaça de Catalunya is the **Rambla dels Estudis** (or **Rambla de Canalets**); then the **Rambla de Sant Josep;** next comes the **Rambla dels Caputxins;** and finally the **Rambla de Santa Monica;** all are collectively called, simply, the Rambla. The top of the Rambla begins just across the street from the Plaça de Catalunya.

2. The Hotel Scene

There are many hotels along the length of the Rambla; only the most noteworthy are included here. In addition to these, there are numerous others where you can find a good night's sleep at a variety of prices, bearing in mind that the price/quality ratio will certainly apply. In Barcelona, and along the Rambla, you can find a room for $15 a night, but it will be dark with a narrow bed, a dirty sink, and a dubious bathroom down the hall. Since the street is busy 24 hours a day, most of the better hotels along its length have installed double-paned windows to block out the constant sound of human and vehicular traffic. If you don't mind having the Rambla waiting for you every time you step outside, these hotels can be great places to stay. And, if you get a room overlooking the Rambla and a little noise leaks through your window, the diversion of watching that street will surely compensate for it. Most of the hotels listed here can be faxed from the States. Also included are hotels off the Plaça de Catalunya, all of which are within a few minutes' stroll from the Rambla. Hotels have parking unless otherwise specified.

Duques de Bergara★★★ (11 C Bergara, Tel. 301-5151, Fax 317-3442). Located a half block from the Plaça de Catalunya, it has beautiful, high, carved mahogany doors with leaded glass and a marble staircase leading out of the lobby. There are 56 modern rooms. There is a restaurant in the hotel. Business conveniences. $120, single; $135, double. Breakfast buffet.

Le Meridien Barcelona★★★★ (111 La Rambla, Tel. 318-6200, Fax 301-7776) is a lovely hotel near the top of the Rambla with 208 large, comfortable rooms. Guests particularly like the radiant heat in the floors of the ample bathrooms. The suites offer personal computers. Walk out the front door and you are on one of the greatest pedestrians boulevards in the world. Inside the rooms are suitably quiet. There are two restaurants on the premises. Business conveniences. $150-250, single; $180-300, double. Breakfast buffet.

Rivoli Ramblas★★★★ (128 La Rambla, Tel. 302-6643, Fax 317- 5053), with its top of the Rambla location, can guarantee that if you stay here you're not likely to be bored. There's something going on outside, 24 hours a day. This hotel has 87 modern rooms, and some of the suites have personal computers. The rooms are quiet. There is a good restaurant in the hotel, a small fitness center, and a rooftop terrace. There is no parking. Business conveniences. $140- 200, single; $160-225, double. Breakfast buffet.

Royal★★★★ (117 La Rambla, Tel. 301-9400, Fax 317-5053) is another fine Rambla hotel, close to the Plaça de Catalunya with 108 comfortable, quiet rooms. The staff is competent and there is a good restaurant in the hotel. Business conveniences. $135-150, single; $150-175, double. Breakfast buffet.

ApartHotel Citadines★★★ (122 La Rambla, Tel. 412-7766, Fax 412-7421) is centrally located smack dab in the middle of the Rambla. Part of a French chain, this new apartment/hotel complex has 131 rooms and apartments, each of which has a kitchenette with an electric oven, dishwasher, and refrigerator, as well as all the amenities of any nice hotel. There are washing machines and dryers on the hotel premises. Business conveniences. $85, single; $100, double.

Atlantis★★★ (20 C Pelayo, Tel. 318-9012, Fax 412-0914). This hotel opened in April 1991 and offers 42 comfortable rooms with modern decor and an attentive staff. It is only half a block from the Plaça de Catalunya. Business conveniences. $100, single; $115, double. Breakfast buffet.

Catalunya Plaza★★★ (7 Plaça de Catalunya, Tel. 317-7171, Fax 317-7855). This hotel opened in July 1992 for the Olympics and is right on the Plaça de Catalunya. Its 46 rooms are comfortable, with ample bathrooms. There is a beautiful high, painted ceiling in the lobby, left over from the 19th century when this was a private residence of one of Barcelona's aristocratic families. There are 14 exterior rooms with a view of the plaça. Business conveniences. $120, single; $140, double. Breakfast buffet.

Continental★★★ (138 La Rambla, Tel. 301-2570, Fax 302-7360). Located near the top of the Rambla, this hotel is popular among tourists, receiving high marks for its friendly staff and safe, secure atmosphere. The 35 rooms are comfortable and five of them have balconies overlooking the Rambla. No private parking. Breakfast buffet. $60, single; $80, double.

Lleo★★★ (22-24 C Pelayo, Tel. 318-1312, Fax 412-2657) is a block away from the Rambla and right next door to the Hotel Atlantis. You looks 'em over and you takes your pick. The hotel's 80 rooms are comfortable, with everything you might need. Business conveniences. No private parking. Breakfast buffet. $100, single; $115, double.

Montecarlo★★★ (124 La Rambla, Tel. 412-0404, Fax: 318-7323). This hotel sports a beautiful foyer with a high ceiling and marble floor, as well as huge mirrors. Old world charm to the max. There is also a lovely sitting room off the lobby with a high, wooden beam ceiling. Centrally located on the Rambla with 80 fully equipped rooms. Business conveniences. Breakfast buffet. $90, single; $115, double.

Ramblas★★★ (33 La Rambla, Tel. 301-5700, Fax 412-2507). This is a charming hotel near the foot of the Rambla. Although the neighborhood is slightly dubious, the hotel is fine—completely safe—with 70 exceptionally comfortable rooms, 30 of which have a view of the Ramblas and 30 with a view of Montjuïc. The best view, however, comes by taking the elevator to the ninth floor, then walking up the stairs to your right. Once on the roof, go to the Montjuïc side and you have a perfect view of the roof of Gaudí's Palau Güell, one of the great roofs in the western world. Business conveniences. No private parking. Breakfast buffet. $75, single; $95, double.

Regina★★★ (4 C Bergara, Tel. 301-3232). This hotel is part of the Best Western chain and offers 105 comfortable rooms in an elegant hotel right off the Plaça de Catalunya. It is popular among business people from other parts of Spain and Europe. There is a restaurant on the premises. Business conveniences. No private parking. Breakfast buffet. $95, single; $120, double.

Cuatro Naciones★★ (40 La Rambla, Tel. 317-3624, Fax 302-6985). This hotel with 34 rooms is right off the Plaça Reial. The rooms are clean and plain, and the same can be said of the bathrooms. There is a restaurant on the premises. There is only local television and there is no air conditioning or private parking. Continental breakfast. $60, single; $68, double.

3. Restaurants and Cafés

This is not the best part of town in which to do some serious dining, but it is, after all, Barcelona, so you know that food and drink are not far away. The slightly overpriced **Café Zurich,** just across the street from the top of the Rambla, is a traditional place for both locals and foreigners to meet. Consequently there are always people sitting there watching the street, waiting for someone to show up for an appointment. *Note:* In late 1996, the Zurich was closed and the block it stands on demolished to make room for a large office/retail complex scheduled to open in 1998. The developers have promised that the Zurich will reopen.

Barcelona's equivalent of reasonably priced fast-food sandwiches, considerably more tasty than the American version, are available at **Pans & Company,** 125 La Rambla, to eat in or take along with you. Sausage sandwiches on *pa amb tomaquet* and a variety of beers are available at the **Vienna Café,** 115 La Rambla, and two blocks further down on the same side of the street is **La Boqueria** market. Inside is a small bar with a half-dozen stools; it is called **Pinocchio's.** Its appearance is not prepossessing, and you may have to elbow your way to the bar to get your order taken, but the daily lunch specials are tasty and the place is favored by people who like to eat.

Located in the midst of all that fresh produce, they turn out wonders on a small stove. Despite the working-class look of it, Pinocchio's is not particularly cheap. Lunch with a glass of wine will probably run you around $15.

Further along, at 79 La Rambla, is the **Egipte Restaurant.** They have a daily menu featuring standard Catalan food at moderate prices. Both this one and its sister restaurant with the same name one block back in the Raval serve consistently good food and they have a menu in English.

Across from the Liceu is the **Café de l'Opera,** which offers an adequate menu of sandwiches and drinks, but is most notable for its 1920s art deco style. It is a café from times gone by, and a nice place to take some liquid refreshment.

From this point on, as you descend the Rambla, a number of cafés have tables in the middle of the promenade. The food and drink at these outdoor tables tends to be a little overpriced, and you may be bothered by the occasional passer-by asking you for some small change, but this is also a great vantage point from which to watch people pass by on La Rambla while taking a little something. Caution: Do not set your bag, packages, or camera down in the empty seat next to you at the table. It could be snatched and gone before you know it.

On the next block, for those who like basic Middle Eastern fast food, is the **Pita House,** where such things as falaffel and shwarma are served at low prices. Just beyond, on your left, built on opposing corners of the C Ferran, are two temples to American fast food, a **McDonald's** and a **Kentucky Fried Chicken.** If you want to bite into something a little more familiar that comes on a bun instead of pita bread, here's the place to do it. There is a very nice restaurant in the Plaça Reial called **La Quinze Nits** (6 Plaça Reial, Tel. 317-3075). It has tablecloths and menus in English, with a range of standard Catalan dishes that are cooked well and reasonably priced. There's an upstairs from which you can eat and look out over the plaça. The *carpaccio de atun* (raw tuna, cut in thin slices and marinated), and *filete* (filet mignon) are both particularly tasty. Reservations are not accepted, and the place tends to have a line out front for both lunch and dinner, so you might want to get there early or be prepared to wait. Of course, the Plaça Reial is far from being the most unpleasant place in the world to wait half an hour for a table.

4. Sightseeing

The Rambla not only has four differently named sections, but is also divided into turfs. While this division is less formal than the street's names, and the street is numbered continuously from top to bottom, its territories are evident. Beginning at the top of the Rambla by the entrance to the metro at the Catalunya station, the first segment of staked-out turf belongs to an ever-shifting group of older men who carry on a perpetual *tertulia,* the Spanish word for a get-together-and-discussion group. The subject of their tertulia varies, mostly being wherever the conversation happens to lead, from the current fortunes of the el Barça soccer team to those of the socialist party, but this is where the old men gather as surely as they gather in town squares across the southern United States to spittle and whittle. Below these men on the right as you descend the Rambla is a drinking fountain. This is the Canaletes fountain, of which it is said that if you take a sip from it you'll come back to Barcelona. The water is as harmless as everywhere else in Barcelona, and tastes just as bad, but if it brings you back to the city it's probably worth holding your nose and having a sip.

There are many ways to walk down the Rambla, and they range between a brisk pace and a relaxed saunter, but one of the best ways to get a first impression of it is by being completely still, something you can achieve by taking one of the metal chairs arranged in ranks just below the fountain. These comfortable metal seats on both sides of the promenade are rented for less than 50 ptas. (25 cents). You sit down and the man will come over and collect the fee from you, and then you are free to sit there as long as you want. It's a remarkably cheap seat at the best spectacle in town. Almost everyone in Barcelona walks the Rambla from time to time, and the parade is interesting at any time of the day or night. When you feel as if you're ready to join it, simply stand up and insert yourself into the flow (keeping a hand on any bags at all times).

Although the number-one sight to see on the Rambla at any given time of day or night is the other people walking there, it also has some notable things to look at. Among them are the **Farmacia Nadal** at 121 La Rambla, on your right side as you descend, with its fancy mosaic tile front; it has been a pharmacy since 1850.

At 116 on your left is the **Generalitat Llibreria,** full of books relating to Catalunya and Barcelona, most which are in Catalan. Nevertheless, it's an interesting bookstore to browse through.

On the other side of the street is the towering outer wall of the **Esglesia de Belén,** which runs down to the C del Carme, where the church's main entrance is located (open from 8 A.M. to 8 P.M. daily). A Jesuit church, it was built originally in 1553 but burned in 1671. Reconstruction began in 1680. Its interior is classic Catalan gothic. The church was burned again during the Civil War in 1936 but was rebuilt in line with what it had been before the fire.

As you continue walking down the Rambla, it's easy to see that the next stretch belongs to the bird sellers whose colorful kiosks offer a wide variety of feathered pets for sale. They range from pigeons to cockatiels, parakeets to parrots. When the sun goes down, so do the metal shutters over the front of the kiosks, and passing by at night one hears the rustling of avian bodies shifting in restless sleep on their roosts.

After the fauna comes the flora—the flower vendors offering seeds, flowers, and potted plants from their kiosks. These stay open far into the night. This was, during the 19th century, the only place in Barcelona to buy fresh flowers, and each flower vendor was the site of an ongoing tertulia, where night after night the same friends would gather to talk and smoke.

At 99 La Rambla, on your right, is the **Palau de la Virreina.** The palace was built at the command of the viceroy of Peru and named for his wife. Finished in 1778, the construction and architecture was overseen by the architect and sculptor Carles Grau. The ample interior patio leads to twin staircases. The most notable of the interior rooms is the dining room with its vaulted roof and its roccoco decorations. The other rooms are considerably simpler, decorated with murals in the "imperial" style. The palau also houses the extremely useful offices of the **Informació Cultural,** where a wide range of information about current cultural offerings in the city is available in a number of languages. The people who work here are extremely helpful and speak English. Next to their office is the colorful **Casa Beethoven,** which sells sheet music.

Down a little way on your right is the *Mercat de Sant Josep* ("Market of Saint Joseph"), known to one and all as **La Boqueria.** This huge market, covered by a sprawling structure of iron, was built in the 19th century. It is the biggest of nine such markets spread throughout the city, and as you will see on entering it, a lot of Barcelonese like to do their shopping in these markets. It's not hard to see why. There is a remarkable abundance of food here from both the earth and the sea. While the Cathedral may be the heart of Barcelona, the Boqueria is its stomach, and it is worth taking a little time to stroll through the aisles of the market. Particularly remarkable, especially for those of us who hail from inland places, are the stalls offering seafood and fish, of which there is a remarkable variety. A walk through the Boqueria is best done before 2 P.M., when many of the vendors close. Almost all of the people working there will have been on the job since before sunrise when trucks arrive in great numbers to unload meat and produce. The market is closed on Saturday afternoons after 2 P.M. and on Sundays.

There are a number of tiny bars inside the Boqueria, and these are good places to stop and have a little something, particularly around 11 A.M. or noon. This is an excellent place to try the traditional Catalan snack of *pa amb tomaquet* (*pan con tomate,* in Castilian), tasty Spanish bread smeared with the juice of fresh tomatoes and sprinkled with olive oil. Anytime you ask for a sandwich in Catalunya, they will ask you if you want the bread *amb tomaquet;* if you say yes, this is what you get on your ham or cheese or tuna sandwich. (If you like tomatoes and olive oil, a resounding *sí* is the recommended response.) In the back of the market, should you feel the call, are rest rooms where for 15 ptas. you can relieve yourself.

Back out on the Rambla, walk a little further down and you will come to a large circular mosaic set in the pavement, which was done by the great Catalan artist Joan Miró. The building across the street, with the umbrellas and dragons affixed to its facade, is the **Casa Bruno Quadras,** built in 1888, whose Oriental exterior was designed to coincide with the Oriental theme of the World's Fair, called the Universal Exposition, held that year in Barcelona.

Further along on the right is the spectacular **Gran Teatre del Liceu** opera house. Despite a relatively plain exterior, the interior was sumptuous on a scale matched only by Milan's La Scala. It was built in 1844 by architect Miquel Garruga i Roca and was constructed to hold 4,000 people (including standing room). In 1861, it burned and was reconstructed on an even grander scale by Garruga's former assistant Josep Oriol i Mestres. The most ornate section, the boxes, were not in place until 1883. From then on, a season's subscription to the opera at the Liceu was *de rigueur* for any Barcelonese aspiring to the upper rungs of society, and the same families continued to occupy the same seats and boxes for generations.

In early 1994, misfortune struck again. An errant spark from a workman's soldering gun started a fire which gutted the Liceu. Work immediately began to rebuild it as it was before, and the grand opening is scheduled for late 1997, which will mark the opera house's 150th year. All reports indicate that it will be every bit as opulent as its former self.

On the other side of the street, just past the C Ferran, is a short passageway leading into the **Plaça Reial.** The plaça was constructed in 1848 to house a Capuchin convent. The fountain in the middle, the Fountain of the Three Graces, was installed in the late 1800s. The lovely lampposts were designed by Antoni Gaudí while he was still a young man, long before he undertook the Sagrada Familia. This plaça has long been a refuge for poor travelers, particularly students, with its abundant hostels. During the 1970s and 1980s it was also the center of Barcelona's small-time drug sellers. The police have gone a long way toward cleaning it up, and it is generally safe day or night, but do not turn your attention away from a handbag or a camera as it will disappear into thin air.

If you go back out to the Rambla and continue your descent, you will pass the new university, the **Universitat Pompeu Fabra** (the Pompeu Fabra University) on the left. It has done much to bring new life and a concentration of young people to the lower end of the Rambla.

On the right coming down the Rambla is the C Nou de la Rambla, the narrow street which houses the **Palau Güell,** designed by Antoni Gaudí (see further description under the Raval district). A little further on is yet another ex-convent, the **Convento de Santa Monica,** which has been turned into a lovely exhibition space for contemporary art and photography. Across the street from it, at number 4-6, is the **wax museum** (open every day 10 A.M.-2 P.M. and 4:30 P.M.-8 P.M; admission is 800 ptas. Tel. 317-2649), one of Barcelona's aging tourist attractions. It has recently brought itself up to speed by inaugurating an exhibit featuring the work of famous European designers on its figures.

At the bottom of the Rambla is the port, with its tall statue of **Christopher Columbus** pointing out to sea.

This 200-foot high Columbus statue (Tel. 302-5224), which marks the end of the Rambla, was built for the Universal Exposition of 1888. For a small admission charge ($1.50), you can take an elevator almost to the top of the statue—it stops at the crown beneath Columbus's feet—for an extraordinary view. The elevator goes up every day but Monday. It can take only four people at a time, so you may have to wait in line for a while. On your right is **Reials Drassanes,** where there was a royal shipyard in the 13th and 14th centuries, and where there is now the **Museu Marítim** (the "Maritime Museum," Tel. 318- 3245) (see the "Raval" section for further description).

That's a general ramble down the Rambla. On the way you'll pass all manner of folks, including lots of living statues up on pedestals who make their living holding a motionless pose until someone pays them to change it. This form of street theatre seems to flourish along the Rambla as nowhere else in all the world. There are also sidewalk performers of every stripe. God only knows what else you may encounter in the way of surprising sights. Up and down the Rambla are also scattered large kiosks with newspapers, magazines, and pornography from all over the world that are open 24 hours a day. If you need an *International Herald Tribune* late at night or early in the morning, this is where you'll find it.

5. Sports

Spectator sport has been replaced on the Rambla by participatory sport. The huge old fronton where the Basque game of jai-alai used to be played in front of a wagering public has been converted into a public sportsplex/gymnasium. The **Fronto Colon** (18 La Rambla, Tel. 302-3295, open 9 A.M.-10 P.M. weekdays, 9 A.M.-6 P.M. Saturdays, 2 P.M.-6 P.M. Sundays) has a small swimming pool, gymnasium, weight room, indoor track, and sauna, available to both men and women. There is a one-day usage fee of 600 ptas. for those who are just passing through. Membership costs about $30 a month. There used to be two big, cavernous frontons, nearly across the street from one another. The second, across La Rambla and up a couple of blocks, stands empty at this writing, awaiting as inspired a use as has been made of the Fronto Colon.

6. Shopping

The shopping here is far from the world-class venues offered in other parts of town. Not too far down from the top of the Rambla, on the left-hand side as you descend, at 120, is a store called **Sepu,** open 10 A.M.-9 P.M., Mon.-Sat. A relative newcomer to its address, it is the local equivalent of a discount department store in the States. Nothing very elegant, but what it sells is serviceable and comes at a considerably lower price than its equivalent in the city's tonier shops. If you want to see the kind of consumer goods that poorer Barcelonese buy for their homes and themselves, this is a good place to do your research.

The most predominant form of shopping available on the Rambla is the lowest common denominator in souvenir shopping. There are blocks that seem to have nothing more than souvenir shops, selling Barcelona T-shirts and innumerable official souvenirs of the Barcelona football club, FC Barcelona, known to its huge numbers of adoring fans as el Barça. Coffee mugs, postcards, ash trays, and a large variety of keepsakes and gee-gaws are also offered for sale in these places.

The **Herboristeria Ballart** (1 C Vidre, Tel. 301-0193, open weekdays, 9 A.M.-1:30 P.M. and 4:30-6:30 P.M.) is an herb and herbal tea shop that has been operated by the Ballart family in this same corner of the Plaça Reial since 1823, and it is worth going in for the smells alone.

For tasty pastries, and the pleasure of entering through a beautiful mosaic-tiled doorway (the place dates from 1820), try the **Christian Escriba Patisseria,** in the *Antigua Casa Figueras* ("Old Figueras House"), at 83 La Rambla.

On Sundays from 10 A.M. to 2 P.M. there is a **stamp and coin market** held in the Plaça Reial.

7. Nightlife and Entertainment

The tiny, triangular, wood-paneled cocktail bar named **Boadas** (open noon-2 A.M., Mon.-Sat.) is wedged in at 1 C de Tallers (Tel. 318-9592), right beyond the corner where the street comes in close to the top of the Rambla, on the right-hand side going down. It was begun in 1933, the first Barcelona cocktail bar, by Miguel Boadas who had learned how to mix cocktails as a bartender in Havana's famous Floridita bar. His daughter has carried on the tradition. It is a favorite among many Barcelonese.

Barcelona Pipa Club (the Barcelona Pipe Club, 3 Plaça Reial, Tel. 302-

4732) is a curious place on the second floor of a building in the Plaça Reial. There are tobacco pipes displayed in cases on the walls of its quarters, which houses a comfortable bar, a small room filled with a short pool table, another pair of salas that serve as pipe museum display sites, and a small room with a few tables and a stage for jazz performances. The bar occasionally features some of Barcelona's best players. There's an admission charge of 500 ptas., with which you become a member of the club for one evening.

Jamboree (17 Plaça Reial, Tel. 301-7564) is one of the historic locations for jazz in Barcelona, a small, cavernous, downstairs nightclub that's still going strong with live jazz every night, followed by a DJ playing rock and salsa for dancing.

Los Tarantos (15 Plaça Reial, Tel. 318-5966), is set back under the arches of the Plaça Reial and is traditionally where many tourists have come for a dose of flamenco. This music, as Spanish as jazz is North American, the soul music of Spain, has its roots in Andalusia and has not been wildly appreciated in Catalunya. Recently, however, flamenco has been gaining an audience among younger Catalans, and by 1996 it was considered something of the thing to do on a weekend to go hear some flamenco. The performances at the Tarantos are often by second string flamenco singers, but even listening to an average flamenco singer can be an unforgettable experience for someone who has had little chance to experience the depths of this music. Los Tarantos generally features rock and roll played for a young set who comes to dance until midnight, when the locale converts itself to flamenco.

Sidecar (in the corner of the plaça at 4-6 C Heures, Tel. 302-1586) is one of the Plaça Reial's older watering holes and places to dance. During the early evening hours it is fairly tranquil, but it heats up as the night progresses, often with bands and theatre groups offering some kind of performance. When the music is playing it's elbow to elbow on the dance floor.

Teatre Poliorama (115 La Rambla, Tel. 210-2458) was purchased by the Generalitat in 1984 as a headquarters for the Catalan theatre company directed by Josep Maria Flotats. Catalan theatre can be quite good and well mounted, but if you don't speak the language, you may find most of it a little tiresome.

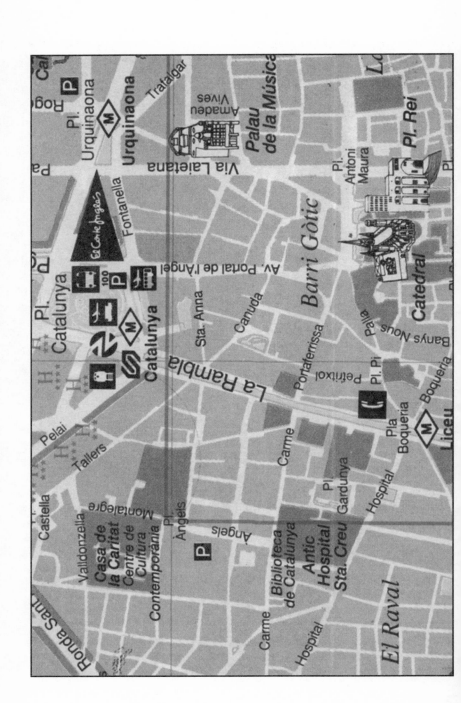

4

The Barri Gòtic

1. Orientation

The Roman city of Barcino is thought to have been founded in the first century B.C. on a slight rise called the Mons Taber. The center of this settlement is marked by a round millstone in the pavement of C Paradís, between the Cathedral and the Plaça Sant Jaume. The Romans put up the city's first walls five hundred years later during the fourth century. The Roman city has never been abandoned but has simply been incorporated into the newer barri gòtic, usually by building on top of the Roman streets and incorporating the higher parts of the Roman walls. There are still Roman ruins visible in a number of points throughout the medieval neighborhood. Any trip around the Barcelona of the Middle Ages will also intersect with the city as it was under Roman rule.

Medieval Barcelona was built first within the old Roman city of Barcino, and then around it, becoming the barri gòtic (barrio gotico in Castilian), the second largest continuously occupied medieval district in Europe next to Prague.

Its narrow cobblestone streets—many with laundry hanging off the balconies above them—wind throughout the barrio. Often in such a street one gets the sense of how it would have been on the same street, in the same spot, eight hundred years ago.

Barcelona prospered as a medieval power and port, as did other Mediterranean cities like Venice and Genoa. While there were hard times and widespread hunger and plague still visited the city from time to time, many a Catalan fortune was made from the city's access to the sea. Barcelona grew so much that the old Roman walls were clearly too confining, so in the thirteenth century Jaume I began construction of a second set of walls for the city, an urban infrastructure project that would take more than a hundred years to complete. When done, the fortifications marked the limits of the barri gòtic. Basically, the barri gòtic ranges from the port to the Cathedral.

2. The Hotel Scene

Almirante★★★★ (42 Via Laietana, Tel. 268-3020, Fax 268-3192) is a relatively small establishment with ample, large rooms—76 of them—that is located close to the Plaça Sant Jaume and the Cathedral. The bathrooms are luxurious and the service is excellent. There is a restaurant in the hotel. Business conveniences. $170, single; $200, double. Buffet breakfast.

Colon★★★★ (7 Av. de la Catedral, Tel. 301-1404, Fax 317-2915) is a nononsense, comfortable kind of place, with a spectacular location—directly across the plaza from the Cathedral. It is popular with business travelers and has 147 rooms. Ten rooms on the sixth floor have terraces, three of which face the Cathedral. There are also a few rather narrow and unappealing rooms. The hotel has a restaurant. Business conveniences. $125, single; $165, double. Breakfast buffet.

Gran Hotel Barcino★★★★ (6 C Jaume I, Tel. 302-2012, Fax 301-4242) is located conveniently just a block in one direction to the Pl. Sant Jaume, and in the other to the metro stop Jaume I. The hotel was opened in 1996 and has 53 comfortable rooms with all the things you would expect. Business conveniences. Breakfast not included. There is less reserved parking for guests than needed, so you may not get a place. $115, single; $142, double.

Metropol★★★ (31 C Ample, Tel. 310-5100, Fax 315-4011) is in an extremely central location, close by the Esglesia de la Mercè and only a couple of blocks from the main post office. The 68 comfortable rooms feature all the amenities, and the staff is helpful and friendly. Business conveniences. $85, single; $110, double. Breakfast not included.

Hotel Rialto★★★ (42 C Ferran, Tel. 318-5274, Fax 318-5212). A half-block from the Pl. Sant Jaume, toward La Rambla, this hotel has 140 rooms and puts you square in the middle of the barri gòtic. Business conveniences. $71, single; $90, double. Breakfast not included. Parking costs an extra $18 a day.

Hotel Suizo★★★ (12 Pl. de l'Àngel, Tel. 310-6108, Fax, 315-3819). A sister hotel of the Rialto, this hotel faces the Via Laietana, just across from the steps for the Jaume I metro station. It has 50 rooms and a staff that is helpful and speaks good English. Business conveniences. $71, single; $90, double. Breakfast not included.

Hotel Gotico★★★ (14 C Jaume I, Tel. 315-2211, Fax 310-4081) is also between the metro Jaume I and the Pl. Sant Jaume. This one is a little cheaper than the others, but equally comfortable. It has 82 rooms and provides parking. $60, single; $72, double. Breakfast not included.

What makes the **Jardi**★★ (1 Pl. Sant Josep Oriol, Tel. 301-5900, Fax 301-5958) a favorite among budget-conscious travelers is its location, in the heart of the barri gòtic, right beside the Plaça del Pi. While the rooms are fairly small, they have been recently renovated and they are clean with adequate bathrooms. Most of the rooms have adequate windows, although not all. Those with a view of the Plaça Sant Josep Oriol are stupendous. There is no air conditioning or television in the rooms, nor is there any private parking or business conveniences. $65, single; $85, double. Continental breakfast.

3. Restaurants and Cafés

The **Brasserie Flo** (10 C Jonqueres, Tel. 319-3102) is a block or two up from the actual barri gòtic, close by the spectacular Palau de la Música, and is a branch of a successful Parisian restaurant. It is done in the style of a brasserie from the 19th century, offering good meat and fish dishes, with a specialty in seafood. The lamb chops are good off the meat side and just about anything from the seafood side of the menu will be excellent. Their seafood sampler plate is a particularly pleasant and filling way to get a taste of the many pleasures awaiting the seafood lover's palate in Barcelona. Open daily from 8:30 P.M. to 1 A.M. Reservations recommended. It's expensive, but the prices are justified by the quality of the food.

Casa Culleretes (5 C de Quintana, Tel. 317-3022). Located just off C Ferran, on a street which is a block in from the Rambla, it is one of Barcelona's oldest eateries. This moderately priced, picturesque restaurant was founded in 1786 and is going strong after two centuries. The food is fine Catalan fare, prepared with fresh ingredients in a relaxed atmosphere steeped in history. Particularly recommended for starters are the *escudella*, a meat and vegetable soup. The menu of the day is generally trustworthy. This is a favorite lunch spot for Barcelonese, so there may be a wait. Reservations recommended. Open 1:30-4 P.M. and 9 P.M.-midnight.

Agut d'Avinyo (3 C de la Trinitat, Tel. 302-6034) is a lovely restaurant in the barri gòtic with more than one level available for dining. It has whitewashed walls and plank floors and serves an excellent and expensive menu of Catalan specialties, any one of which can be generally counted on to be stellar. Closed Sundays, Easter week, and August. Open 1-4 P.M. and 8 P.M.-midnight. Reservations are required for both lunch and dinner.

La Bona Cuina (12 C de la Pietat, Tel. 315-4156) is located just behind the cathedral and is strong on interior decor, almost modernista with its dark wood walls, lace curtains, and huge art nouveau mirror dominating the room. It has menus in a variety of languages and serves up a moderately priced array of Catalan specialties, doing a particularly good job with fish and seafood. Reservations recommended. Open daily 1-4 P.M.; 8 P.M.-12 A.M.

Dive (Tel. 225-8158) is a recently opened, Hollywood-inspired franchise in the Maremagnum at the port. It is part of a chain designed by director Steven Spielberg and features items taken from his movies. It has a submarine decor and a big dinosaur from *Jurassic Park* out front. The moderately priced menu has both stateside specialties like burgers and fries and some Catalan dishes like *escalivada* (grilled eggplant, red pepper, and onion). There is a full restaurant on the ground floor of the Maremagnum, with a large bar and tables upstairs. The bar level is open from 1 P.M. to 1 A.M.; the restaurant, 1 P.M. to 4:30 P.M. and 8 P.M. to midnight. Open seven days a week. Reservations recommended.

Brasseria Insolit (Tel. 225-8178). Located in the port's Maremagnum, opposite the Dive, it has an excellent and reasonably priced restaurant downstairs, with some nice views across the port and a lovely outdoor terrace. Both grilled meats and seafood are worth trying. Upstairs, owned by the same people, is the **Bar Internet,** with six computer terminals that you can e-mail home from, or explore the Internet on. The terminals cost 600 ptas. for a half-hour's use, or 1,000 ptas. for an hour.

Quatre Gats ("The Four Cats") (3 C de Montsió, Tel. 302-4140). The first one was a café opened in 1897 by two Catalans: painter Santiago Rusinyol and novelist Ramón Casas. It was the center of Barcelona's turn-of-the-century creative world. Picasso was a frequent visitor and had his first show here. The present edition of this café, located off the Av. Portal de l'Angel just above the barri gòtic and the plaza of the cathedral, is the third, but it is still located in the impressive modernista building designed by Josep Puig i Cadafalch. The main dining room is impressive with art nouveau lamps and wrought iron tables with marble tops. On the second floor, there's a balcony with small tables where couples can sit and eat while looking down on the dining room. The menu features Catalan specialties. The food is good and the ambience and service are both marvelous. A meal with wine will be around $30 per person. Closed Sundays for lunch. Open 1:30 P.M.-midnight. Reservations recommended.

Los Caracoles (14 C de Escudellers, Tel. 302-3185) is located a block west of the Plaça Reial, in a neighborhood where it's a good idea to exercise normal security precautions—but it is still well worth exploring. It's a big draw for tourists, but locals also have a healthy respect for the restaurant's substantial, solid, Catalan cuisine at a moderate price. For a change of pace try *los caracoles* (snails), for which the place is named, or you may want to sample one of the chickens being charbroiled over hot coals on rotisseries beside the front door. The neighborhood may be shabby, but the restaurant's interior has lovely tilework and a cheerful decor. Open daily 1 P.M.-midnight. Reservations recommended.

La Fonda (10 C de Escudellers, Tel. 302-3152). Just up the street toward the Rambla from Los Caracoles, this lovely restaurant with its clean lines and large plate-glass windows is owned by the same people who own Las Quinze Nits in the Plaça Reial, and the food is the same reasonably priced, well-prepared Catalan cuisine. They have a menu in English and do not take reservations. There's often a line, so be prepared to wait your turn. It's worth it. Closed Mondays. Open 1-4 P.M. and 8:30-11:30 P.M.

Celta Pulperia (16 C de la Mercè, Tel. 315-0006) has a very long bar and a few tables. The tapas consist of seafood like *pulpo gallego* (octupus sprinkled with paprika) and are displayed along the bar. Don't fill up, though, because in the next block on the left are a trio of dark bars, each featuring hard cider and a strong, pungent cheese called *cabrales,* which takes over where gorgonzola leaves off. With a plate of cabrales served on bread and a glass of hard cider to wash it down, lovers of strong cheeses will think they've died and gone to heaven.

El Gallo Kiriko (19 C Avinyó, Tel.: 412-4838) is a Pakistani restaurant that features a dirt-cheap selection of different kinds of couscous. In the evenings they have a small back room that they open up. You walk through the front room, past the bar, and into a cave-like space with a substantial section of Roman wall. It's probably the only place in town where you can dine beside a wall of old Barcino (in addition to this remarkable decor, the couscous is pretty good, too). Open daily except Mondays, 1 P.M.-1 A.M. No reservations.

La Pallaresa (11 C de Petritxol, Tel. 302-2036). This is a *xocolateria,* and just like it sounds, it specializes in hot chocolate, but the version here is a far more rich and creamy one than what you might be used to stateside. It's also a good place to try an horchata, and its location by the Plaça de Pi guarantees that there will be an interesting crowd. Open daily 9 A.M.-1:15 P.M. and 4-9 P.M.

El Xampanyet (22 C de Montcada, Tel. 319-7003), on the same street as the Picasso Museum and wedged in among a group of medieval palaces, is a gem of a tiny bar. Operating in the same place since 1929, it's a superb place to sample Barcelona's typical tapas offerings, accompanied by a strong glass of cold *sidra fresca* (fermented apple cider). The tapas are lined up on the bar, and while anchovies are the specialty of the house, served with some crusty bread, anything you pick will be tasty. Closed Sunday evening, Mondays, and during August; open noon-4 P.M. and 8-11:30 P.M.

Govinda (Tel. 318-7729). This restaurant is located right by the Rambla, just off the C de la Canuda at 4 Plaça Vila de Madrid. An ample salad bar and tasty daily specials make this moderately priced vegetarian Indian restaurant a favorite among locals and visitors alike. In addition to the ever-changing entrees, the desserts made with yogurt and fresh fruit come highly recommended. Closed Sundays and the month of August. Open 1-4 P.M. and 8-11 P.M.

Bunga Raya (7 C Assaonadors, Tel. 319-3169). Turn left off the C Princessa on C de Montcada and take a right at the first block. This is the only place in town to get an inexpensive and toothsome Indonesian meal. The rice dishes are delicious, particularly when heated up with some of the fiery and tasty *sambal ulek,* ground chili pepper paste mixed with lime juice that is served as a condiment. It has limited space and is frequently crowded. At the moment they don't accept reservations, but it would be worth it to call and see if that has changed.

Gelateria Italiana Pagliotta (between C Trompetes and the Pl. de l'Àngel at 15 C Jaume I, Tel. 310-5324). Italians are respected almost as much for their know-how with ice cream as for their touch with pasta, and this is considered by many to be the best ice cream parlor in the city. If you're counting calories, there is also sugarless ice cream here. Closed between Oct. 15 and March 1. Open 9 A.M.-11:30 P.M. daily.

Set Portes (14 Passeig de Isabel II, Tel. 319-3033) is another of the city's venerable dining institutions. It is between the port and Barceloneta. The name means "seven doors," and it extends for half a block, set back under archways. It is a sprawling, happy bistro, opened in 1836. It is a favorite among tourists and has its share of faithful local diners as well. The reason for that is their seafood. They have a multilingual menu and they won't bat an eye if you come in at 10 P.M. and ask for a paella, although locals consider that quintessential Spanish dish to be something one eats at midday. Open daily with nonstop service from 1 P.M. to 1 A.M. Reservations recommended.

4. Sightseeing

One good place to begin when visiting the barri gòtic is the Metro station Jaume I, on the Via Laietana. Standing at the top of the stairs leading up from the station, facing out, take a right and walk up the C de Jaume I to the **Plaça Sant Jaume.** You are walking up the Mons Taber, as the Romans knew it, the first real climb after leaving the port. The area was within the Roman walls, and the two principal roads of the Roman city passed through the plaza, el Cardo, which is presently C del Bisbe to the northwest and C de la Ciutat to the southeast, and el Decumanus, presently the C de Coll to the southwest and C de la Llibreteria to the northeast. The Plaça Sant Jaume has been the administrative heart of Barcelona and Catalunya since the Middle Ages. It is also the place where citizens have traditionally gathered to express either pleasure or displeasure with their political leaders. On the left is the **Casa de la Ciutat,** Barcelona's city hall. The building is also known as the *ajuntament,* because it is from here that the city is governed. The facade facing the Plaça Sant Jaume is 19th-century, neoclassical architecture. However, if you walk along the side of the building on the C de la Ciutat, you will see the original gothic facade from the 14th century. The building itself is open to the public at this writing on Saturday and Sunday between 10 A.M.and 2 P.M. Otherwise, and unless you have some business with executives of the ajuntament, or can present the plausible appearance of having such, you will not be admitted.

The building was a private house when it was bought by the municipal council in 1372 to serve as city hall. Alongside of it was the Església de Sant Jaume, originally built in 985. The house was expanded and the **Saló de Cent** ("Council of One Hundred") was built. The elegant chamber is still used for meetings and conferences at the ajuntament. The current principal entrance dates from 1847 and is an excellent example of neoclassical architecture.

Across the square is the **Palau de la Generalitat,** the Palace of the Catalan government. Built in the 15th century to house the medieval Catalan parliament, the building now houses the executive branch of Catalunya's government, including the office of the president. The building has some breathtaking rooms, including the astounding 17th-century vaulted **Capella de Sant Jordi** ("Chapel of Saint George") with a huge mural of Saint George slaying the dragon. The generalitat is not open to the public. The single exception is the day of Sant Jordi (Saint George, Catalunya's patron saint) in late June, when the public is allowed to tour the building. Should your visit coincide with this date, do not miss the opportunity to see inside the medieval building, but come early because there is always a long line of citizens who want to take a look at where their taxes are spent.

The building's origins were in two houses on the C de Sant Honorat that had belonged to Jews before antisemitic mobs murdered or expelled the city's Seferad in 1391. Jewish property was bought for a song from fleeing Jews, or simply taken when its owners turned up dead or went missing. (There were no Jews living again in Barcelona until the 20th century.) The houses were acquired by the generalitat in 1403 and expanded in 1418. In 1526, further building was undertaken, and an outdoor staircase was built to a second floor of gothic gallerys and the patio of oranges, an open-air

patio planted in orange trees. Under Franco, when the generalitat was out-
lawed as a governing body, the Diputacion Provincial was installed here.
Since 1977 it has once again belonged to the generalitat. The primary
entrance from the Plaça Sant Jaume dates from 1597 and is in an Italianate
style, done with Genovese marble.

Facing the principal entrance to the generalitat, the narrow, medieval
street to its right is the C del Bisbe. If there's a beautiful, delicate arched
walkway bridging the street about half a block along, you're in the right
place.

Turn right at the C de la Pietat and walk along the back wall of the **Catedral de Barcelona,** often called *La Seu* by Barcelonese because it is dedicated
to Saint Eulalia, one of the city's patron saints, who died a martyr at the
age of 14 in the year 304 A.D. In a minute we'll visit the cathedral, but for the
moment let's follow the sinuous turnings of that back wall.

You'll come to a cross street, the C dels Comtes. Carry on for another
half-block and you'll be in the Plaça del Rei ("King's Square"). This small,
beautiful plaza is surrounded by a complex of buildings that made up the
Palau Reial Major ("Great Royal Palace") constructed in the 14th century
on 12th-century foundations, which were, in turn, built on part of the original Roman city. It served as a palace for the counts of Barcelona who ruled
the Catalan-Aragonese confederation. For this reason, the city is still called
the *ciutat condal,* the "city of counts." Should you have the good fortune to
be visiting during the week-long celebration called the *festa de la mercè* in
mid-September, there are often free jazz concerts held here in the evenings,
and the acoustics are superb (come early to grab one of the scarce seats).

The building at the back of the plaza is a wall of the great palace. On
the right, facing it, there rises the austere stone of the **Palatina Chapel.** On
the left is the **Lloctinent Palace.** This plaza was, for centuries, also a market
for animal feed and straw. Archeological excavations revealed a cemetery
beneath the plaza, dating from the earliest years of Christianity's presence
in Barcelona. The broad stairway on the right leads up to the *Saló de Tinell*
(the "Dining Hall").

Here you need to purchase a ticket for 500 pts. that will allow you to
visit the entire complex of the **Museu d'Història de la Ciutat,** which includes
the Palau, a sizeable exhibit of the Roman ruins beneath the city, and the
lovely **Casa Clariana-Padellàs.** The Museu (located beside the Plaça del Rei
at 2 Plaça del Veguer, Tel. 315-1111, Fax 315-0957) is closed Mondays and
open Tue.-Sat. from 10 A.M. to 2 P.M. and 4 to 8 P.M., except between June
and Sept., when it is open from 10 A.M. to 8 P.M. It is also open Sundays
from 10 A.M. to 2 P.M.

First, the Saló. This huge room—110 feet long and over 50 feet high—is
crossed by six giant arches spanned by wooden beams. Legend has it that it

was here that Columbus presented himself to Ferdinand and Isabella on his return from his first trip to the Americas, and the room contains a painting rendering the scene with Columbus surrounded by American Indians, being interviewed by the "Catholic monarchs," as the royal couple were called. In the same part of the Palau as the Saló is the lovely vaulted **Capella de Santa Agata** ("Chapel of Saint Agatha").

From here, go back down the steps and across the plaça to the entrance marked Barcino. Here begins a fascinating tour of an actual excavated part of the Roman city, which was called Colonia Iulia Augusta Faventa Paterna Barcino. Included in this subterranean tour are the remains of several Roman houses, as well as the basilica and baptistery where the first Christians gathered from the fifth century onwards. At the far end of the subterranean portion of the tour, you will exit in the C del Veguer in the 16th-century **Casa Clariana-Padellàs,** the Gothic house of a 16th-century merchant. Here, be sure to ask for the free brochure published by the city, in English, called *Itinerary through Roman Barcelona,* which offers its own walking tour of many of the accessible sites with Roman remains.

Walk back toward the Plaça del Rei, and retrace your steps toward the Cathedral. When you reach the C del Comtes, look to your right; a block down you will see the entrance to the **Museu Frederic Marès** (Plaça de Sant Iu, 5, Tel. 310-5800). This museum, located in a section of the Palau Reial Major and established with funds provided by the sculptor Frederic Marès, houses a collection of medieval art, particularly sculpture, donated by him to the city. Upstairs there is a display of artifacts from everyday life in Barcelona, which range from pipes to purses to toiletries to coins. There is an admission charge and the museum is closed Mondays. Open Sundays and holidays 10 A.M.-2 P.M.; other days, 10 A.M.-5 P.M.

If you continue along the C de la Pietat, you will pass the C Paradis on your left. At number 10 is the most impressive remainder of the Roman city of Barcino: four huge fluted columns with Corinthian capitals mounted on a podium. These are from the eastern rear corner of the Roman temple of Augustus, dedicated to the cult of the emperor in the first century B.C. It was also the site of the Roman forum, the center of the city.

Back on the C de Pietat you will come to a door into the **Catedral de Barcelona,** on your right, which leads into the cloister, a charming courtyard with a garden of orange, magnolia, and palm trees, a fountain, and a pool, where there is a resident gaggle of white geese. Some of the chapels around the cloister have interesting murals and figures. The fine screens and the gates that enclose the chapels were done with forged iron in the 1300s. From the cloister, you can enter the cathedral through the **Capella de Santa Llúcia** ("Saint Lucy's Chapel"), where it was the custom up until recent times that on Dec. 13, the Day of Saint Lucy, the blind, whose patron saint she is, would gather in great numbers in the cloister.

Once inside, the monumental size of the cathedral becomes evident. This Gothic cathedral was built on the site of two earlier cathedrals, and was begun in 1298 during the reign of Jaume II. The earliest work, which begins by the door of Sant Iu, was done in a transition style from the Romanesque to the Gothic. The apse was covered in 1310, and between 1317-1338 work was directed by Jaume Fabre. The central altar, of marble, was consecrated in 1337. The wooden altarpiece is from the 15th century. In 1390, construction was begun on the choral nave. It was essentially completed by the mid-15th century, but its facade and spired cupola were not added until the end of the 19th century.

The cathedral has three naves, each with four bays, their arched ribs coming to a point. The remains of Sant Iu (Santa Eulalia) herself, are contained in a marble crypt in front of the *Altar Major* ("High Altar"). Behind the altar is the stone sarcophagus of the saint, a piece of alabaster worked by a sculptor from Pisa, Italy, whose name has been lost to time. The sarcophagus dates from 1327 and is crowned with a virgin and four angels. The third chapel beyond the crypt, the *Capella de Sant Benedicte* ("Chapel of Saint Benedict"), is the most remarkable of the cathedral's numerous chapels for its nine-panel *Altarpiece of the Transfiguration,* done in the 15th century by the Catalan artist Bernat Martorell. Don't miss the 15th-century polychrome tomb of Sant Ramon of Penyafort. The chapel of Christ of Lepanto, with a vaulted roof 65 feet above the floor, was done between 1397 and 1405 by Arnau Bargués. Its central object is a life-size sculpture in wood of the crucifixion, carved around 1300.

The enclosed choir (for which there is an admission charge) has wooden stalls from the 14th and 15th centuries which display the coats of arms of the Knights of the Golden Fleece. The cathedral also has a museum (Tel. 315-1554), open daily from 11 A.M. to 1 P.M., which has an admission charge. Among the museum's exhibits are a gold throne that belonged to a 15th-century count of Barcelona, as well as a number of reliquaries and altarpieces.

Leave the cathedral by the front door. It is here, in the **Plaça de Sant Iu,** in front of the cathedral, that Catalans gather on Sundays between noon and 2 P.M. to dance the *sardana,* the traditional dance of Catalunya, accompanied by drum, flute, and brass instruments. It's a slow dance of people holding hands in a circle, which appears deceptively simple but actually requires dancers to pay close attention. The dance is believed to have its roots far back in antiquity, in early Greek civilization or before. Its present version was pretty much worked out in the 19th century. The sardana is taken seriously by young and old alike as a reaffirmation of their Catalan heritage, and it is a pleasure to watch them come together to carry on the traditions that bind them.

PLAÇA DE SANT FELIPE NERI

Standing outside the cathedral, facing away from it, turn left and walk across the plaça. On your left you will see the Roman gate of the Plaça Nova. This section of the Roman wall dates from the first century A.D.; the two cylindrical towers were put there for defense. If you walk through it, up a short hill, you will be back on the C del Bisbe. Take a right at the C Montjuïc de Bisbe and walk back along this winding, one-block street to the Plaça de Sant Felip Neri, a lovely little peaceful square beside the cathedral of the same name. It has a gentle fountain in the middle beneath two overhanging acacia trees. On one side of the plaza, at number 2, is the **Museu d'Història del Calçat** ("Museum of the History of Footwear") (Tel. 301-4533). It is a two-room collection that includes sandals worn by a first-century slave, as well as a variety of examples of shoes in history, and the footwear of the famous. Open Tue.-Sun. and holidays 11 A.M.-2 P.M. The church is a typical counterreformation church, finished in 1752, with a neoclassical altar that is decorated with angels of polychromed wood.

PLAÇA DE PI

Go back to the entrance to the Roman gate and take the C de la Palla on your left. Just after you leave the plaça, on your left is a well-preserved section of the Roman wall. There are several semicircular windows that were added during the Middle Ages. At the base of this wall flowed one of the Roman sewers.

Bear right at the fork and continue along the C de la Palla and you will come into the **Plaça Sant Josep Oriol.** This is a good place to stop for some refreshment at one of the outdoor cafés, if you can find a seat. This plaça is always full of folks, both tourists and Barcelonese, and has a delightful feel to it. On the far side of the plaza is a wall of the **Esglesia de Pi** (the Church of the Pine). Until the 19th century the Plaça Sant Josep Oriol was the parochial cemetery. A church that was in this spot, but was not this cathedral, figures in 10th-century documents that refer to a church built in a new part of the city, just outside the Roman walls. However, remains of that church have not been found. The present cathedral was begun in the early 1300s and finished in 1453. The interior is typical of Catalan cathedrals of the time with one nave and lateral chapels. Its ceilings are over 40 feet high. Some of the windows are quite old, such as the one in the left span from the side door, which was done by the painter Antoni Viladomat at the beginning of the 18th century. The painter's remains are in a small chapel in the church. Close to the sacristry entrance is a gothic tomb resting on two lions that is the final resting place of Arnau Ferrer, a patron of the church who died in 1394.

When you're ready to continue, follow the wall of the church around to the **Plaça del Pi,** passing in front of the church. It was in this plaza where for many years a huge pine grew that gave the cathedral its name. Take the C del Cardenal Casañas for one block to La Rambla. On your left at number 16 is a house that dates from the fifteenth century. After a block you will come out at the Rambla and the Liceu metro station.

THE ROMAN WALLS

Barcino was the Roman city founded in 15 B.C. The medieval city, then the modern city, buildings in the barri gòtic were frequently constructed on top of it. Many a person in this neighborhood setting out to remodel a kitchen or bathroom turns up a stretch of Barcino's walls, and while a considerable amount has been uncovered, plenty of the Roman city still waits beneath something else to be rediscovered. It was small, covering some 10 hectares (almost 25 acres), and laid out in a regular fashion with parallel and perpendicular streets. The best examples of this are in the ruins beneath the Museu d'Historia de la Ciutat, but there are numerous other Roman remains in the area.

Among the places to see are some impressive sections of the defense wall from the late Roman empire that run parallel to the Via Laietana below the C San Jaume on the C Sots-tinent Navarro. Continuing down to the end of this street, one can turn right at its end and come to the Plaça dels Traginers with a small shady plaza and a few benches from which you can gaze on a circular tower that defended the eastern corner of Barcino. From here walk straight on to the C Regomir, turn right, and a half-block later turn right again up the alley beside the **Centre Civic Pati Llimona.** Go inside and visit their lower level, which has a section of a Barcino street and was the site of important Roman baths—speaking of which, there are free bathrooms here for those who feel the need.

From here walk westward to the C Avinyó. Further up, across the C Ferran, at C Banys Nou, 16 is a building housing a center operated by the generalitat for physically challenged children. Inside is a wide expanse of Roman wall, as well as the relief of a pair of legs and feet which was built into the wall. This is one of the most remarkable of the Roman ruins currently visible. The teachers who work with the kids are glad to have visitors, but they ask that you call ahead to the center (Tel. 318-1481) to fix a time to come and look so that your presence can be integrated into the children's day.

SANT PERE AND THE PALAU DE LA MÚSICA

This is the neighborhood just above the barri gòtic. It was contained within the second city wall built during the Middle Ages. In the direction of the Plaça Urquinaona is the part of Barcelona that began to be densely populated during the tenth century and was brought within the city's perimeter in the thirteenth. After that, it served as the center of Catalunya's textile industry during the centuries it prospered. Currently, the most outstanding thing to see in the district is the **Palau de la Música.** Going up the Via Laietana, a couple of blocks above the Cathedral, take a right on C Sant Pere Més Alt and you'll see it at number 2. It is surely one of the most amazing concert halls in the entire world. While Gaudí is the best-known representative of the turn-of-the-century modernist movement in Barcelona architecture, an equally great member of that group was Lluis Domenech i Muntaner, who did this building. It is a striking example of pure modernist work. The building was completed in 1908 and has a stained glass dome. While its exterior brick and mosaic is worth seeing in itself, it is the interior that boggles the mind.

The Palau was recently renovated and it was a job well done, restoring the palau to a gleaming newness without detracting from any of the remarkable work inside. It is a huge building with lines that capture the eye and send them soaring. In the concert hall 18 half-mosaic, half-relief figures representing musical muses come forward from the back of the stage, and on one side huge carved horses gallop out into the air.

There is colorful mosaic everywhere, and it a remarkably otherworldly building. Gaudí is said to have referred to it as what heaven must be like. The acoustics are not fantastic, but the ambience more than makes up for it. In addition to regular performances of the Barcelona Symphony Orchestra, numerous musical events are staged here, ranging from piano recitals to Emmylou Harris concerts.

There are two good ways to see the inside of the palau. One is to go to a concert. If you can't get to a concert there are guided tours for about $2 that begin at 3 P.M. on Tuesday afternoons, for which you must reserve a place in advance by calling 268-1000.

LA RIBERA

From the mouth of the Jaume I metro station, instead of turning right and going toward Plaça Sant Jaume, turn left and cross the Via Laietana. Walk down the C Princesa to the **C de Montcada,** the second street to the right.

Despite being only a couple of blocks long, the C de Montcada holds six palaces from the late Middle Ages. They generally conform to a common style of Mediteranean urban palace—an imposing entrance patio and stairs leading to the main rooms on the first floor—and are closely packed together. Endlessly altered over the years, most contain features from several periods. During the 13th and 14th centuries, this was a very exclusive part of Barcelona. This also accounts for the nearby **Cathedral of Santa Maria del Mar.** While not as spectacular inside or out as the Cathedral of Barcelona, this has traditionally been the cathedral that is closest to the hearts of the people.

The first of the palaces one reaches on C de Montcada is the **Palau Aguilar** on the left at number 15, currently the home of the **Museu Picasso** (Tel. 319-6310, 315-4761; Fax 315-0102), part of which was built as early as the 13th century. The museum also has occupied a second palace next door at number 17, the **Palau de Castellet.** The artist was born in Malaga and spent most of his life in France, but he was a student in Barcelona.

The museum's collection contains mostly early work and lithographs, although Picasso himself donated some 58 works to the museum when it opened in 1963. There are also some fine examples of Picasso's ceramic work. It is closed on Mondays; open 10 A.M.-8 P.M., Tue.-Sat. and holidays; and open 10 A.M.-3 P.M. on Sundays. There is an admission charge except on the first Sunday of each month.

Across the street at number 12 is one of the finest and largest palaces, now the **Museu Tèxtil i d'Indumentària** ("Clothing and Textile Museum") (Tel. 310-4516, 319-7603). It has textiles from the fourth century to the present day, and a fascinating collection of garments from the past three centuries. There is a small café with a few tables outside on the patio in the courtyard, where you can sit and sip something surrounded by the palace's 14th-century walls. The museum is closed on Mondays, open Tue.-Sat. from 10 A.M. to 5 P.M., Sun. and holidays from 10 A.M. to 2 P.M. There is an admission charge.

At number 19 is the **Palau Meca,** which is currently used as a cultural center. If you're interested in a glass of cider and a succulent tapa, take a breather at number 22, **El Xampanyet.** Next to it at number 20 is the **Palacio Dalmases,** a relative latecomer built in the 17th century and currently the headquarters of an organization promoting Catalan culture.

Across the street at number 25 is the **Palacio de los Cervelló,** from the 15th century, where there is currently a **Galeria Maeght** offering beautiful art books and prints for sale and revolving shows in its exhibit space. On your left, just before you reach the Passeig del Born, will be Barcelona's narrowest street, **C de las Mosques** ("Street of the Flies"), which is currently closed with a barred gate on either end. The street, as can be seen through the gate, is not wide enough for an adult to lie across.

Carry on to the end of C de Montcada and you will be at the Passeig del

Born. On your left, at the end of the Passeig, is the huge, covered, former **Born Market,** now used for a variety of events like book fairs. There it stands, the beautiful glass and iron ex-market with its immense arched iron beams and no one in city government has figured out quite what to do with it. On your right is the beautiful Basilica of Santa Maria del Mar, the favorite church of the citizens of Barcelona. Art critic Robert Hughes wrote of it in his book, *Barcelona:* "There is no grander or more solemn architectural space in Spain."

The cathedral of Santa Maria del Mar was begun in 1329 and finished remarkably quickly, for a building of its size and grace, in 1384. It is built over a burial site that dates back to the first century A.D. It is a towering and profoundly solemn cathedral, with beautiful acoustics. Its columns are the widest apart of any Gothic church in Europe, some 43 feet. Two ranks of gracefully proportioned colums rise into the fan vaults. There is some remarkable stained glasswork in the cathedral, with the most notable being the rose window above the main door, done in the 15th century. Like the more cluttered and less affecting Cathedral of Barcelona, it lacks the pinnacles found on northern Gothic churches and has gargoyles that bristle out horizontally from its heights.

Across from the end of the C de Montcada, on the other side of the Passeig del Born, is the C de la Vidrieria. Cross the C de l'Esparteria and note the **Pastisseria La Mallorquina** on your right, where they have been making mouth-watering pastries since 1878. You will come out in the Plaça de les Olles. On your left is a clean and attractive café, with only bar seating, called **Cal Pep** (Tel. 310-7961). This is an excellent and reasonably priced place for fish and seafood dishes, and it is open 1-4:30 P.M. and 8-12 P.M., Tue.-Sat. They do not take reservations.

Cross the Av. del Marqués de l'Argentera. A half-block on your left is the **Estació de França,** where international trains arrive and depart. Should you need a public restroom, this is a good place to find one. Just beyond it is the **Parc Ciutadella,** the only large downtown park in the city, which has been there since 1869 (for further description see "Barceloneta" section). This is also the site of the somewhat seedy **Barcelona Zoo.**

ESGLESIA DE LA MERCÈ

One block below the Plaça Reial is the restaurant **Los Caracoles.** Turn left here and go along the C del Escudellers. You will come to a lively, open plaça with a striking wood-and-aluminum sculpture by Leandre Cristoful, a contemporary Galician sculptor. The plaça was recently named in honor of the British writer George Orwell, whose book *Homage to Catalonia,* about his experiences fighting in the Spanish Civil War for the Republican side (and his time spent in Barcelona), is a favorite here. Carry on across the plaça. On your right is the C de Carabassa. In the course of its two blocks you will pass beneath two wrought iron steel bridges crossing the street, and you'll come to the C Ample. Take a right, walk half a block, and cross the plaça on your left in front of the **Esglesia de la Mercè** ("Church of Our Lady of Mercy").

Tradition has it that the Virgin appeared in the dreams of three men, including the king, Jaume I, instructing them to found a monastic order that would be dedicated to redeeming the numerous Christian captives held by North African pirates. The order's first church was finished in the plaça in 1267. It was reformed between the 14th and 15th centuries, and in the 17th century, a convent was built next to it in the building still standing. The Virgin of the Mercè is the patron of Barcelona, and many people here are fervently dedicated to her. Before Franco's death and the decline in the Church's influence, championship sports teams would come here to recite Hail Marys to the Virgin.

The facade is deceptively simple. Inside is a typical Baroque church, with one nave and lateral chapels. The Virgin was carved by Pere Moragues in 1361, and the Christ child was sculpted in 1561. There is an impressive vaulted ceiling with stained glass. Take a left as you come out the church door and another left when you get to the C de la Mercè that borders the plaça. The streets aound the Cathedral were, at one time, home to some of Barcelona's richest families, but the area has been abandoned by the wealthy for more than 500 years. Little has been done to it, and this is another of those streets that gives a pedestrian the sensation of having traveled back in time a couple of centuries. There is a beautiful wrought iron bridge overhead on the C de la Mercè that joins the church to the former convent. The C de la Mercè runs three blocks north into the C de la Fusteria at the Plaça Antonio López and the main post office.

THE PORT

For most of Barcelona's history, the port has played a critical role in the city's economic well-being and sense of itself. But during the 20th century, the port took on the aspect of a dingy collection of warehouses and railroad tracks. That's no longer the case. The 1992 Summer Olympics have come and gone, but they left the port and the city's seaside transformed forever. It used to be said that 20th-century Barcelona was a city that had turned its back on the sea. That is certainly no longer the case. Across the traffic circle from the Colom statue a large mall, **Maremagnum,** has been built at the end of a broad pedestrian pier. It is a collection of fashionable shops, fast-food restaurants, bars and cafés. It is also the site of a movie theatre with eight screens, an IMAX cinema, and Europe's largest aquarium. Across the water from Maremagnum is another long pier, scheduled to be the site of a World

Trade Center, expected to open in late 1997 with commercial, office, and convention space. Maremagnum curves around from the foot of the Rambla to Barceloneta, the neighborhood that is traditionally the home of the city's fishing families. The cityside edge of the mall is bordered by a street called the Passeig de Colom, which runs from the left of the Colom monument along the waterfront to the mosaic sculpture by North American sculptor Roy Lichtenstein across from the post office. Beside the Passeig de Colom is the **Moll de la Fusta** ("Wood Quay"). This walkway was the first sign of redevelopment at the port and was built in 1989, five years before ground was broken for Maremagnum. It features a string of pavement bars and restaurants, including Javier Mariscal's wacky **Gambrinus** bar, with its giant fibreglass lobster on the roof. Prices at places along the Moll de la Fusta are higher than most other cafés, and this has not become a particularly popular place to go, except late at night when its discos attract a substantial number of young people. However, Maremagnum and the Olympic Village complex of beaches and cafés created beyond Barceloneta have made the seaside a favorite destination of locals year-round.

5. Sports

Let's face it, sports are not the big draw to the barri gòtic. The best sport to practice here, and it's one of the best cities in the world in which to practice it, is walking.

6. Shopping

At number 2 C del Bisbe you'll see an unusual shop, **La Antigua Cereria de Luis Colima** (Tel. 315-0954), which offers a wide variety of products made from wax, including votive offerings in the shape of skulls. Next to it is **2 Bis,** an interesting odds-and-ends store with a number of whimsical pieces of artisanship as well as some lovely glassware and plates.

The entire area around the Cathedral is the center for Barcelona's trade in antique books and maps, and there are numerous stores where you can search for the treasures that attract you. The **C de la Palla** is one of the city's premier streets for antiques, and there are a number of interesting stores along it selling antique books and maps. One of them is on the right at number 33, the **Libreria Trallero.** For ceramics, take a look at **Arturo Ramón** at 25 C de la Palla. For furniture, paintings, and porcelain you looks 'em over and takes your pick, but **Alberto Grasas** comes well recommended at 10 bis C de la Palla.

There is an **antiques market** held every Thursday from 10 A.M. to dark in the Plaça del Pi, which draws a sizeable number of both buyers and sellers.

La Manual Alpargatera (7 C d'Avinyó, Tel. 301-0172). This store, close to the C Ferran between the Ramblas and the Plaça San Jaume, sells hand-made espadrilles, cloth shoes with rope or straw soles which are more comfortable and durable than you might think, although they're less than adequate in the rain. They come in a variety of styles and colors and they're made here in the back room. It has been open since 1910. Among the many satisfied customers have been Jack Nicholson and Pope John Paul II. Open Mon.-Sat., 9:30 A.M.-1:30 P.M. and 4:40-8 P.M.

Calçats Solé (7 C Ample, Tel. 301-6984). This is a terrific shoe store, just across from the Plaça de la Mercè, near the port, where they make their own. They have a wide range of sandals, many in traditional forms from various parts of the country. They also make fancier shoes. The clerks are helpful and friendly.

Itaca (26 C Ferran, Tel. 301-3044) offers a wide and reasonably priced selection of glasswork and pottery, featuring pieces by artisans from all over Spain. If you're planning on taking a piece home with you, be sure to tell them; they will wrap it well to protect it on the trip.

Joan Grau (6-8 C de la Vidrieria, Tel. 319-4046). This shop is run by the fifth generation of the Grau family to deal in glassware, including bottles, vases, and drinking glasses. The business was founded in 1850, and there is a back room with an exhibit of antique glassware that is not for sale. These folks are experts at packing delicate items to travel long distances. Open weekdays 9 A.M.-1 P.M. and 4-8 P.M., and on Saturdays 9 A.M.-1 P.M. Just across from the end of the C de Montcada and close by the Santa María del Mar Cathedral, in a street whose origins reach back to the medieval glass trade.

Alifa Cosmètic (14 C Princesa, Tel. 319-6093, Fax 319-7423). This is a cosmetics store for people of Hispanic or African descent. Dark-skinned people often have trouble buying beauty products in Europe, and this is the first store of its kind in Barcelona. It opened in 1996 and stocks a wide range of cosmetics, grooming aids, wigs, falls, and hair products. Open 9:30 A.M.-1:30 P.M., Mon.-Sat.

Fira de Productas Naturals ("Natural Products Fair"). Two days a month, the *Collectiu de Catalunya* ("Collective of Catalunya") brings its members together in the Plaça del Pi, where they set up booths and offer their wares. These range from honey and chocolate to goat's cheese, as well as non-edibles like bee's wax candles. Open the first Friday and Saturday of each month, 9:30 A.M.-8 P.M.

Cereria Subira (7 C Llibreteria, Tel. 315-2606). This is the oldest store in Barcelona; it began life in 1761 selling ladies clothing in this location just off the Plaça Sant Jaume. Currently it offers just about every kind of candle you could imagine. Open 9 A.M.-1:30 P.M. and 4-7:30 P.M., Mon.-Fri., and 9 A.M.-1:30 P.M. on Saturday.

Sombrereria Obach (2 C de Call, Tel. 318-4094). Run by the Obach family for many years at this location not far from the C Avinyó, the store offers every kind of hat you could think of to put on your head, from traditional men's dress models to berets to Barça soccer team caps. If hats are your thing, this is a must stop. Open Mon.-Sat., 9:30 A.M.-1:30 P.M. and 4-8 P.M.

7. Nightlife and Entertainment

Harlem Jazz Club (8 C de Comtessa Sobradiel, Tel. 310-0755). Just off the C de Avinyó, this is a sit-down-and-listen venue and one of the best places in town to go for jazz, although it's small. The first set usually begins around 11:30 P.M., but the sound system and the choice of recorded music they play on it is excellent, so it's a pleasant place to wait. No cover charge.

Irish Winds (Tel. 225-8187) is an excellent example of the kind of Irish pub style that has been repeated in a number of venues in Barcelona. This one is on the top floor of the Maremagnum, and on a summer evening the terrace is a lovely place to sit with a Guiness in hand. A large, predominantly English-speaking crowd. Open 11 A.M.-4 A.M. Mon.-Thur., 11 A.M.-6 A.M. Fri. and Sat.

Blue Note (Tel. 225-8003). Mixed in with the terrace cafés, fast-food restaurants, and flashy discos of Maremagnum is this glass-fronted jazz bar on the waterfront with both live and recorded jazz. It costs 1,500 ptas. to get in, which also pays for your first drink. It's in the Maremagnum shopping mall at the port and is open 9 P.M.-2 A.M. Tues. and Wed., 9 P.M.-4:30 A.M. Thur. and Fri., 11 A.M.-4:30 A.M. Sat., and 11 A.M.-2 A.M. Sun.

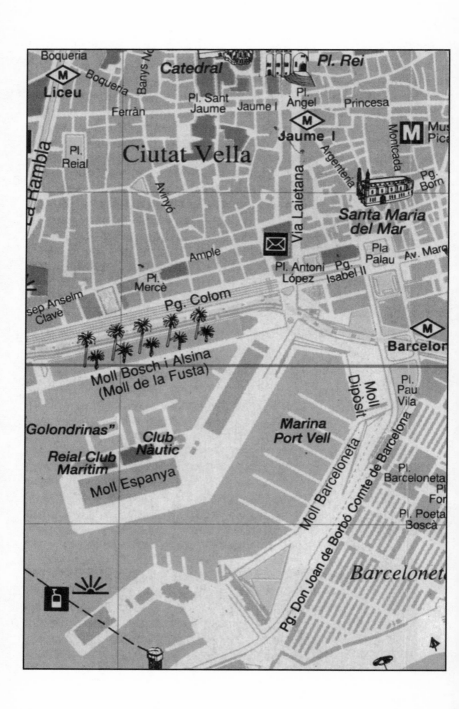

5

The Raval

1. Orientation

The Raval essentially runs up from Drassanes, to the right of the Colom statue at the bottom of the Rambla, and is boundaried by the Rambla, Av. Paral.lel, the Ronda Sant Pau, and the Ronda Sant Antoni. It's a large district, encompassing a number of smaller neighborhoods that have had their own names over the centuries. The area originated during the Middle Ages as a population just outside the walls of the city. It was here that the more unpleasant trades were practiced, such as slaughtering animals, and where the sick were sent to the huge old medieval hospital, still standing between the C de la Hospital and the C del Carme. In the Middle Ages, a trip to the hospital was usually one way. If you were sick enough to go, your chances of ever returning were slim.

All of these areas, including the marketplace that stood in about the same place where the Boqueria market stands today, were brought within the city when a third set of walls was built in the 14th century. A large stretch of these walls is still visible on the lower part of the Av. Paral.lel.

The area was honeycombed with factories, and the workers who toiled in them lived close by. It cannot have been a very pleasant neighborhood in which to struggle for one's daily bread. Its narrow streets and deep shadows, along with its dense and poor population, left much to be desired in the way of sanitary conditions. Whatever rare and exotic diseases arrived in the city through the port usually made their way first to the Raval, as did the sailors themselves. In the 19th and 20th centuries, it was in the Raval where most of Barcelona's radical workers' movements gained their largest followings.

The lower part of the Raval, nearest to Drassanes and the port, has been called the **barrio chino** since a journalist pinned that name on it in the early 1900s. The area has never been home to many Chinese, but the name connoted a low-life port barrio with lots of prostitutes, nightclubs, and drugs. While the police have cleaned the area up tremendously, and the ajuntament has pursued an aggressive policy of tearing down whole blocks of apartments in order to create spaces of light and air, there are still some grey and shabby blocks on which bodies line up to be sold, and passersthrough at night might want to keep a hand on their wallets and purses.

The Raval definitely has a grittier feel to it than the barri gòtic, but it also feels even more lived in and alive. It is the inner city, Barcelona style, and frequently rewards those who wander through its narrow, old streets with some wonderful sights. It is also the most multicultural of Barcelona's districts. This is the part of town where you come to buy curry powder, basmati rice, or yucca. Halal butchers sell meat to the Muslim faithful while next door a carnesseria sells every imaginable part of the pig to Catalans. Most of the Catalan speakers in the Raval are senior citizens who have lived there all their lives, or hip, young couples who are moving back from the more staid parts of the city where they were raised. There are, however, many, many people from other parts of Spain who are there to look for work and live among the Asians and Africans and Latin Americans who make up a large part of the barri's population.

2. The Hotel Scene

San Augustín★★★ (3 Plaça Sant Augustí, Tel. 318-1658, Fax 317- 2928). A comfortable 77-room hotel about three blocks off the Rambla in a small plaça along the C de la Hospital. The street is one of the most international and colorful in Barcelona, where Catalan senior citizens live next door to families from Pakistan, Bangladesh, Morocco, Colombia, or Andalusia. From here it is only a brief walk over to the Rambla. $55-$65, singles; $75-$85, doubles. Buffet breakfast is included. No private parking.

España★★ (9 C de Sant Pau (08001), Tel. 318-1758, fax 317-1134). Built in 1902, a block off the Rambla in the Raval, by the great modernist architect Lluis Domenech i Muntaner, this hotel was awarded a special prize by the city in 1903. It has a beautiful, high-ceilinged, turn-of-the-century lobby, a good restaurant, a helpful staff, and an overall feeling of age. The 84 rooms are adequate and clean, if nothing to write home about. No television (except one in the lobby, and that one is an antique and not hooked up to a satellite), no air conditioning, no private parking. $50, single; $65, double. Breakfast included.

3. Restaurants and Cafés

Egipte (3 C de Jerusalem, Tel. 317-7480 and 79 La Rambla, Tel. 317-9545). Both locations attract a varied crowd of diners from students to artists to tourists who appreciate the long list of Catalan dishes on the menu and the reasonable prices. There are menus in English, the ingredients are always fresh, and the food is good. No reservations. Open daily 1-3:30 P.M. and 8-11:30 P.M.

Casa Leopoldo (24 C de Sant Raphael, Tel. 441-3014). This is another longtime popular favorite among serious Barcelona restaurant goers. Located in a run-down, seedy neighborhood (you may want to take a cab to the door), the tiled walls and sturdy furniture create a truly Catalan decor, and the food is guaranteed to please with its freshness and flavor. The seafood dishes are particularly noteworthy. Reservations recommended. Closed Mondays. Open Tue.-Sun. 1-4 P.M. and 9-11 P.M.

Ca l'Isidre (12 C de Flors, Tel. 441-1139). This place has been around long enough that artist Joan Miró declared it among his all-time favorite places to eat, and it is still going strong. Among the specialties that earned this place a Michelin star are *espardenyes* (a kind of sea slug eaten only in Catalunya) and calf's brains. The restaurant has an excellent wine selection and takes particular pride in its array of armagnacs, that full-flavored cousin of French cognac. Closed Sundays, holidays, and from mid-July to mid- August. Reservations are necessary and it is recommended to make them two days in advance.

4. Sightseeing

Walk through La Boqueria market from the Rambla and exit behind it onto the C de Jerusalem. Should you feel the need for a bathroom break, there are public toilets—a relative rarity—located behind the Boqueria with a minimum charge (15 ptas.). Turn left on the C de Jerusalem, which ends at C de la Hospital. This neighborhood was part of the old Raval, built outside the city's wall that ran along the Rambla.

ANTIC HOSPITAL DE LA SANTA CREU

Take a right, walk two blocks and on your right, at number 56, is the **Antic Hospital de la Santa Creu.** This complex was, for centuries,

Barcelona's medical school and hospital. During the Middle Ages, virtually all of Catalunya's doctors were educated here. The hospital's origins appear to have been toward the end of the 10th century, and in 1024 it was turned into a hospital for pilgrims. Its position outside the walls made it a convenient place to isolate the sick from the well. A number of different hospitals were constructed here to house various patients—people with leprosy, newborn babies and their mothers, etc. Eventually, toward the end of the 14th century, all these were united in one grand hospital complex. The gothic building began to take form as early as 1401, and the glory of it reached even as far as the ears of the pope in Rome. Pope Benedict XIII is known to have sent 10,000 gold florins to help with the project. When completed, it was one of the largest hospitals for the poor in Europe and served as a school of medicine for all of Catalunya. Up until that time, the great majority of Barcelona's physicians were Jewish, because only Jews maintained a university that had medicine on its curriculum.

The complex's facade on C de la Hospital is from the 16th century and features beautifully sculpted gargoyles. The windows are from the 14th century and were brought from an older hospital. The principal door is a pure piece of Catalan Renaissance. Walk through the courtyard. This is known as the "new courtyard" and was added in the 17th century. The next courtyard is gothic and dates from 1417. It actually consists of three different chambers that open onto it beneath simple arches. On your left is the **Casa de Convalecencia** ("House of Convalescence"), which currently houses the **Biblioteca Catalunya** ("Catalan Library"), containing a tremendous number of books and manuscripts dating back to medieval times on nearly every aspect of life in Catalunya.

If you have the gift of gab and a subject you'd like to research from the Catalan perspective, you can talk a Visitor's Pass out of the guard and go upstairs to one of the two great stone halls that serve as reading rooms. They have walls made of massive cut stone blocks and vaulted beam ceilings that arch 30 feet above the tiled floors. Some 15 feet up one wall are tall, leaded, stained-glass windows that illuminate the reading rooms. Up and down the great stone halls, people sit at oak tables in pools of light from the lamps on the table beside them, heads down, reading in pockets of brightness among the medieval shadows of the rooms. You look up your titles in the card catalogue and give them to the librarian, who in turn sends a worker back to find them.

If you continue walking past the entrance to the biblioteca, you will pass on your left a branch of the Barcelona public library system, the **Biblioteca Popular Sant Pau.** This is one that is open to everyone. You can go in, have a seat, and read the latest Castilian and Catalan periodicals if you want to.

Even if you don't read the languages, you might want to go inside, because at the top of the stairs to the right are free public restrooms, and if you look like you might be a library patron no one will object to you using them.

Carry on through the courtyard and on your left will be the simple gothic facade of the hospital, from the 15th century. On your right is the building that housed the Academy of Medicine, constructed in the eighteenth century, and finally, just before exiting into the C del Carme, is an expansion to the hospital from the 17th century, which currently houses the **Institut de Estudis Catalans.** Go through the gate ahead of you and you will step out of the 14th century and into present-day traffic and crowds on the C del Carme.

MUSEU D'ART CONTEMPORANI DE BARCELONA

Turn left, then take your first right off C del Carme, the C dels Àngels. Two blocks straight on will bring you to the **Museu d'Art Contemporani de Barcelona** (the "Barcelona Museum of Contemporary Art," or the MACBA as it is known to Barcelonese) (1 Plaça dels Angels, Tel. 412-0810). An entire square block of the Raval's narrow streets and old, decrepit apartment buildings was razed in order to build the museum, which opened in November 1995. It is built in a large, open plaça, a few blocks into the Raval from the Ramblas just off the C d'Elisabets. This huge white whale of a light-filled exhibit space was designed by North American architect Richard Meier and reflects his allegiance to pure rationalism. The entryway with its vast glass wall allows light to flood the exhibition areas. The gleaming white exterior is something you either love or detest. The permanent collection is drawn from work between the 1940s and the 1990s, and is heavily weighted toward Catalan artists of this period, among them Miró and Tàpies. It also includes work by a small but important group of Europeans such as Klee, Calder, and Dubuffet. In addition to the permanent collection there are revolving temporary exhibits. Closed Mondays. Open Tues.-Fri. noon-8 P.M., Sun. and holidays 10 A.M.-3 P.M. Wednesday is a half-price day. Normal admission is about $5.50.

CENTRO DE CULTURA CONTEMPORÀNIA DE BARCELONA

Behind the center, continuing along the C de Montalegre, is the **Centro de Cultura Contemporània de Barcelona** ("Barcelona Center of Contemporary Culture") with its lovely courtyard, well worth a look inside (5 C de Montalegre, Tel. 412-0781). It has been in use since 1994 as a place where a wide range of cultural events are held, ranging from conferences to exhibitions to performance art to theatre and dance. You can find out what's there by looking in the Cartelera in the daily paper or, if you can make out the Catalan, there's a 24-hour hotline to call for what's happening: 481-

0069. The building itself was, for centuries, a convent and the city's poorhouse, and for that it is still known as the **Casa de Caritat** ("House of Charity"). Closed Mondays. Open Tue.-Sat. 11 A.M.-2 P.M. and 4-8 P.M.

From here it is worth walking a few blocks back into the Raval to see the Romanesque church of **Sant Pau del Camp** (Tel. 310-2390). It's Barcelona's oldest church, built in the twelfth century. Where it stands now hunched in upon itself under a protective dome was once open countryside. Columns on either side of the portal were built using materials from seventh-and eighth-century buildings. It's a squat, low building, completely different from the soaring cathedrals that were to come. At 101 C Sant Pau, closed Tuesdays, open other days 11 A.M.-1 P.M.

Continue on, and at the top of the C de Montalegre, turn right on the C de Valdonzella. Walk a block to the C de Tallers and turn right. This will lead you back to La Rambla.

PALAU GÜELL

To see the lower part of the Raval, a good place to begin is at the intersection of the Rambla with C Nou de la Rambla, a small street on your right, just below the Plaça Reial. Here, at number 9, is the remarkable **Palau Güell** (Tel. 317-3974). This was one of the first important works by the great modernist architect Antoni Gaudí i Cornet, who lived from 1852 to 1926, the year he was struck and killed by a streetcar in Barcelona, the city he had transformed. Gaudí was the most outstanding of the modernist architects who flourished in Barcelona during the end of the 19th century. His work is marked by a plasticity and flow that is rarely achieved in stone. Many of Barcelona's buildings occupy the air in some remarkable way, but no one's creations have the power to make people stop and gasp like Gaudí's.

The Catalan industrialist and political leader Eusebi Güell i Bacigalupi's patronage of Gaudí allowed the architect to build some of his most striking works, and this one is no exception. Gaudí was 34 when he began designing the palace in 1886, and was given free rein by Güell both in terms of design and cost. It was the first time Gaudí had been at liberty to fully express himself and he is said to have worked very hard on it. It is an imposing, somewhat melancholy building, without the light and airy feeling that permeates much of Gaudí's later work. At the heart of the palace is the huge main salon, covered with a parabolic dome three stories above the floor. Another remarkable room is the chapel built for the Güell family within the palace, which features a pair of doors sixteen feet high covered in tortoiseshell—nearly two hundred square feet of it. The chapel was ransacked during the Spanish Civil War and is currently used as a storage space. The most impressive element of the Palau Güell, however, is not to be found inside at all, but rather on the roof. It has 20 conical chimneys, covered with broken tiles in the style known as *trencadis*. Art critic Robert Hughes has called the roof the most beautiful permanent sculptural installation in the city. Unfortunately, it is not open to the public and not included on the standard tour of the palau. About the only way for most people to see it is to visit the Hotel Gaudí on La Rambla and ask to go to their roof, from which there is a lovely view of the top of the Palau Güell. The palau is open for tours Mon.-Sat. 10 A.M.- 1:30 P.M. and 4-7:30 P.M. It currently serves as a research arm of the Institut del Teatre. There's a charge for the tour of about $2.50.

BARRIO CHINO

From here you can continue into the Raval along the C Nou de la Rambla until you reach the Av. Drassanes, where you can turn left and walk down toward the sea. Or you can choose to explore any of the narrow streets that run through the warren of the Raval before you reach Av. Drassanes. This is the area of Barcelona known as the **barrio chino,** and it's the closest thing to a red-light district that the city has to offer. This is not a Chinese neighborhood and never has been. It was baptized in the 1920s by a local journalist who saw a film about vice in San Francisco's Chinatown and applied the name to the Raval's bars and bordellos. Recent years have seen some intensive clean-up campaigns mounted by the police, and prostitution and drugs have been greatly curbed here, but a walk through, even during daylight hours, has a considerably more sinister feeling to it than one gets in other neighborhoods. There are a lot of people leaning against buildings or drinking in bars who look like they are up to no good, or at least wish they were. After dark, this is an area for prudent visitors to avoid.

The Av. Drassanes terminates at the port and the medieval shipyard called **Drassanes.** It was built in the 14th century, and is the largest intact medieval shipyard in the world. It provides us with a wonderful example of what a huge industrial building was like in the Middle Ages. When it was constructed, its slipways opened right to the sea. Over the next six centuries, the city reclaimed some two hundred yards of land that was underwater then, and which is currently between Drassanes and the sea.

It was built as a joint effort between the King of Aragon-Catalunya, the city of Barcelona, and the Parliament, and it was done during the heyday of Barcelona's maritime influence, which in those days stretched past Italy all the way to Greece. That Barcelona was a real Mediterranean power can be seen in the immensity of the shipyards that were built to serve the industry.

Approaching Drassanes from the Rambla, at the right of the Door of Peace, which faces the sea, is the entrance beneath the four towers of Peter II (the Great), the king who initiated the project, and whose son Peter III (the Ceremonious) finished it in 1378. It is his shield that has been sculpted here, and on the right at the corner of the facade is also the shield of the Generalitat. Walking further along the Paseo de Colom, one sees the long parallel bays, made of brick, that were needed to construct ships.

MUSEO MARÌTIMO

These bays are currently exhibition spaces for the **Museo Marìtimo** (Av. Drassanes, s/n, Tel. 318-3245). The collection is an intriguing one that includes maps of the explorers (including one drawn by Amerigo Vespucci), navigational instruments, and models of ancient boats and ships—from the large oceangoing vessels of international Catalan commerce, to the small, workhorse boats that took Barcelona's fishermen to sea. There is a $3 admission charge, $1 for those under 18. Closed Mondays. Open Tue.-Sat. 9:30 A.M.-1 P.M. and 4-8 P.M.; Sundays and holidays 10 A.M.-2 P.M.

Bordering the Raval district on its far side away from the Rambla is the Av. del Paral.lel, which runs down from the Plaça d'Espanya to Drassanes and the port. This is the Broadway of Barcelona. Along its length run music halls and theatres. The cafés and bars sometimes seem to be peopled with characters right out of a Damon Runyon short story. Dancers, gamblers, and show business people make this a lively and slightly seedy avenue, which is not frequently visited by tourists amd has a considerable amount of down-at-the-heels charm.

5. Sports

Sports facilities do not exactly abound in this neighborhood, but there is a covered swimming pool, the **Piscine Folch i Torras** (Plaça Folch i Torras s/n, Tel. 441- 0122), a couple of blocks above C de Sant Pau, located in the middle of the Raval. It is open seven days a week apart from the month of August, when it closes. Mon.-Fri. it's open 8 A.M.-5 P.M.; Sat. 8 A.M.-7 P.M.; and Sun. and holidays 9 A.M.-1 P.M. A one-time usage is 500 ptas., or you can buy 11 visits to the pool for 5,000 ptas.

6. Shopping

The Raval is a crowded residential district, and its shops are mostly those where people come for their daily necessities. Since many foreigners live here, it's also where other Barcelonese come to buy curry, basmati rice, and Arabic and Latin American foods. There are lots of small wholesalers, *Tot a Cien* ("Everything at 100 Pesetas") stores selling knick-knacks, and numerous everyday shoe and clothing stores, but not much to attract serious shoppers. Since the Contemporary Art Museum rose up, however, a number of interesting art galleries have relocated to be close by, a trend that promises to continue. Among them are the following.

Galeria Ferran Cano is right across the plaça from the museum at 4 Plaça dels Àngels (Tel. 310-1548), and it's a big addition to the roster of the area's galleries. A well-known dealer based in Mallorca, Cano often mounts shows of the best young Spanish artists. It's worth going by the gallery to see whose work is up. Open 5-8 P.M. Tues.-Fri. and 11 A.M.-2 P.M. Sat.

Galeria Carles Poy, at 10 C del Doctor Dou (Tel. 412-5945), is the newest version of a gallery that began in the 1980s and that continues to show young, rising artists from Catalunya, Spain, and abroad. Closed in August. Open Tues.-Sat. 10 A.M.-2 P.M. and 4:30-8:30 P.M.

Dou Deu, at 10 C del Doctor Dou (Tel. 301-2940), is a store next to the Carles Poy gallery that sells a wide range of things made by artists whose names you may recognize as well as others who are still struggling. The inventory here is fascinating. It's closed during August; open Tues.-Sat. 10A.M.-2 P.M. and 4:40-8:30 P.M.

7. Nightlife and Entertainment

London Bar (Nou de la Rambla, 34, Tel. 318-5261). It's a deep tunnel with an old mahogany bar and mirrors along the walls, and at the far end there's a stage where a wide variety of music, often jazz, is performed. It's popular with young foreigners. It has been open for a long time, since 1910 in fact, and always been a favorite among the more bohemian population of the city. It's open 7 P.M.-3 A.M. Wednesday through Sunday and doesn't take any credit cards.

Bar Marsella (65 Sant Pau, no telephone). This place may look like it just went up yesterday, but it has been in the same family for three generations, and some of the regulars have been coming in for more than half a century. In addition, it is always full of young foreigners, mostly English-speaking, who are studying or teaching English in Barcelona. There's a tiny stage wedged into one corner and a wide assembly of groups occupies it, frequently paid no more than what a hat passing will raise. Thursday night is drag night, when drag queens strut their stuff and belt out ballads; Sunday night is when classical musicians take over the stage. Open 5 P.M.-1 A.M. No credit cards.

Raval (19 C del Doctor Dou, Tel. 302-4133). This is a wonderful spot. The crowd leans towards artistic and intellectual, and it's a good deal older and more civilized than the foreigners drinking at the Marsella. Downstairs is a tastefully appointed, good-sized room and a lovely bar, while there are more tables upstairs. It is a bar where people can sit and talk, and that's what lots of people come to do. Open from 8 P.M. to 2:30 A.M. No credit cards. It's on a somewhat hard to find block: from the corner of the Rambla and C del Pintor Fortuny, walk into the Raval. The third street to your right is C del Doctor Dou.

Bar Pastis (4 C del Santa Mònica, Tel. 318-7980). This is the best bar in Barcelona for Francophiles. It is close to the port and Drassanes, and was opened by a Catalan couple in the late 1940s who had lived in Marseilles and for many years thrived on the trade of French sailors. These days there's a clientele from around the globe, but everything remains French. You can drink a pastis and listen to the likes of Edith Piaf or Maurice Chevalier. The prostitutes that regularly work the tiny street in front of the bar are transvestites. It's a dubious neighborhood, but the bar's clientele are generally left alone. No credit cards. Open 7:30 P.M.-2 A.M.

Chic Studio (64 Av. del Paral.lel, Tel. 329-5454). This cavernous discotheque with three levels has gone through a number of incarnations with different names, but always with high energy and strong music for dancing until the wee hours on the weekends. Frequently a good place to hear the best salsa and Latin jazz that the city has to offer. Admission charge varies, but it usually begins at around $20, and drinks are not cheap.

La Ovella Negra ("The Black Sheep") (5 C Sitjàs, Tel. 317-1087). Just a few blocks off the Rambla and half a block from the C Tallers, it's a big grotto of a bar with loud music and pool tables. Its cheap prices and boisterous atmosphere are particularly attractive to a college-aged set, both locals and those from abroad. Open daily, 5 P.M.-3 A.M.

La Paloma (27 C Tigre, Tel. 301-6897). This is a dance hall that looks like it came out of the last century, with red velvet drapes and rococco decor. It draws a wide spectrum of people who come to dance to the live music, played by a band that easily swings from tango to cha-cha to samba to waltzes. The young come as do the old who have been dancing here for years. Even if you are not a ballroom or Latin dancer, a trip inside for a drink to hear a set and watch the dancers is well worth it. A generally older crowd attends the earlier sessions. Open Thur.-Sat. 6 P.M.-9:30 P.M. and 11:30 P.M.-4 A.M. It's high up in the Raval close to the Ronda Sant Antoni, a few blocks toward the Sant Antoni market from the Universitat metro stop.

Apolo (113 Nou de la Rambla, Tel. 442-5183). Dancing has always been the key for this address. Long ago it was a dance hall, and that's what it still is. On Saturday and Sunday evenings, there is ballroom dancing during the earlier hours of the evening and the cover charge is $4. However, as the hour wears on, it changes and about midnight becomes a raging discotheque, known for its wild clientele, good music, and anything-goes atmosphere. Open on the weekends until 6 A.M., and occasionally later, there's a cover charge of around $10, and drinks are expensive.

6

Barceloneta and the Olympic Beaches

1. Orientation

There are a number of ways to get to Barceloneta. There are at least four bus lines that pass by from different parts of the city. You can walk there along the Moll d'Espanya, by the water, until you reach the Passeig de Joan de Borbó, or you can take the L4 yellow line of the metro to the Barceloneta station.

This is a barri on a triangular piece of land that stands between the harbor and the sea. It is built on ground that was reclaimed from the sea; the neighborhood, constructed in the early 1700s, has traditionally housed fishing families and those who made their living from the Mediterranean. This is a fascinating neighborhood where people still bring chairs and tables down into the cool of the shady, narrow streets to pass the late summer afternoons sipping something and talking.

Beyond Barceloneta are the new beaches that were installed during the run-up to the 1992 Olympics. There are a number of them, with ample stretches of sand and the occasional palm tree. A green flag at either end of the beach indicates that the water is safe for swimming. If you visit during the summer months, be prepared for the crowds on the local beaches during the weekends. The Barcelonese have taken to their newly opened coastline in a big way, and on the weekend the beaches are packed with sun

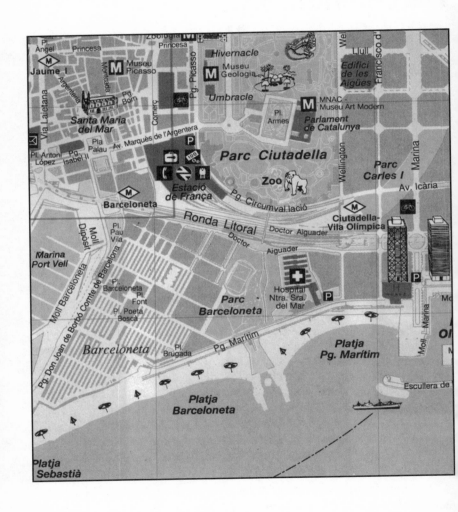

worshippers. Women here often sunbathe topless, as they do all over Spain. On any summer's day there are plenty of women, from teenagers to grandmothers, baring their chests to the rays. However, it's a purely personal choice and many also choose a more modest dress.

2. The Hotel Scene

Hotel Arts★★★★★ (19 Passeig de Marina (08005), Tel. 221-1000, 800-241-3333; Fax 221-1070). This luxury hotel occupies one of two towers constructed beside the Platja Barcelona, a new beach created for the Olympic games. The other tower is an office building. The hotel is owned by Ritz Carlton and the claim is that at 44 stories high, it is the tallest in Europe. There is an elegant restaurant, a café, two outdoor swimming pools, and the Mediterranean 100 yards from your door. Many of the rooms offer stupendous views of both the city and the sea, and the service is everything that it should be. 397 rooms; 56 executive suites; 2 presidential suites. Business conveniences. It's expensive and worth it. $185, single; $220, double. Breakfast buffet included.

Park Hotel★★★ (11 Av. Marquès de l'Argentera, Tel. 319-6000, Fax 319-4519). Across the street and half a block up from the Estació de França, it has 87 comfortable rooms, all with satellite TV and mini-bar, and all of which were renovated in 1990. Business conveniences. $71, single; $104, double. Breakfast included.

3. Restaurants and Cafés

When you visit Barceloneta you would do well to bring an appetite, because this is one of the city's richest troves of restaurants. As you might expect, most of them rise or fall on their seafood dishes, but many of them offer excellent meat dishes as well. From the Maremagnum end of the harbor, around to Passeig Don Joan de Borbó, in the back streets of Barceloneta, and on down the string of beaches, there are numerous good restaurants.

La Gavina (Tel. 221-0595). Even before you get to the Passeig Don Joan de Borbó, if you're coming from the direction of Maremagnum, you can walk along the Moll del Dipòsit behind the Palau de Mar by the water. Here there are a string of nice restaurants where you can dine on the terrace and watch the folks walking by and the yachts moored at their slips. La Gavina offers particularly tasty seafood dishes. You pay for the pleasant ambience—these places are medium-priced to moderately expensive, but the food is excellent. Reservations recommended. Open 1-4:30 P.M. and 8-11 P.M.

Antigua Casa Sol (4 C de Sant Carles, Tel. 221-5012) is an extremely popular place in Barceloneta serving the freshest of fish and seafood. Their menu changes daily depending on what was bought during the morning's dockside auctions. Open daily 1 P.M.-midnight, but closed Saturday evenings, Sundays, and the first two weeks of September. Reservations recommended.

Can Costa (70 Passeig Don Joan de Borbó, Tel. 221-5903, 221-5043) They've been cooking seafood in the Barceloneta neighborhood at this restaurant for more than 70 years, and they do a fine job of it. Their fideuà (pronounced fee-day-wah) is a delicious variation of the standard paella which uses noodles instead of rice. They also prepare an excellent paella. Save a little room for a homemade pastry to finish off your meal. Reservations recommended. Closed Sunday evenings. Open Mon.-Sun. 1-4 P.M. and 8-11:30 P.M.

Can Maj (23 C de Almirall Aixada, Tel. 221-5455) is a little fancier than many of Barceloneta's other fish and seafood restaurants, but the food and service are both consistently good. This is an excellent place to sample a *suqet,* a delicious and filling fish and potato stew. Closed Sunday evenings, on holidays, and during August. Reservations recommended.

El Cangrejo Loco (29-30 Moll de Gregal, Port Olímpic, Tel. 221-1748) One of four lovely restaurants with clean, crisp lines that are located near the Platja Olímpic ("Olympic Beach") on a pier that juts out into the Mediterranean. This is a restaurant that nicely blends traditional fish and seafood dishes with some of its own creations. Reservations are recommended as this place has proven to be especially popular among Barcelonese and is frequently full. There are many seats in these four restaurants that allow you to look out to sea while you dine. Hm, good. Open daily.

Salamanca (34 C de Almirante Cervera, Tel. 221-5033). It's right at the edge of Barceloneta and the beach, so the seafood part of the menu figures to be tasty, but they also specialize in *paradillas* (grilled meats). Reservations recommended. Open seven days a week 1 P.M.-4 P.M., 8 P.M.-midnight

Bar Hivernacle (Tel. 268-0177) is a café/bar under glass beside the immense greenhouse in the Parc de la Ciutadella. It's a popular place to go late on a Sunday morning to read the paper and have coffee. Any visit to the Ciutadella Park should be punctuated with a stop here for the refreshment of both body and soul. It's open from 10 A.M. to 10 P.M. daily.

4. Sightseeing

From the end of the Maremagnum complex closest to Barceloneta, walk along the Moll del Dipòsit and cross over the former Passeig Nacional, now renamed the Passeig Don Joan de Borbó after King Juan Carlos's late father. On your left are the narrow streets of Barceloneta. Take your nearest street back into Barceloneta, C de la Maquinista, go three blocks, and take a right, which will be C del Baluard. Just before the C Escuder, on your right, is the church of **Sant Miguel del Port,** in a charming, small plaza of the same name. The church was completed in 1755 and the facade features sculptures done at that time by Pere Costa. Return to the C del Baluard and follow it to the end, about six blocks down, and you'll get a look at the charm of the Barceloneta neighborhood. These narrow streets and small flats are where generations of sea-going Barcelonese have raised their families. It was built in the last half of the 18th century and has not changed greatly since then. Recently, however, the city has reclaimed much of the actual beachfront, and traffic through and around Barceloneta is increasing tremendously—as is the value of the property it occupies. How much longer Barceloneta will be allowed to occupy its anachronistic grid of 25 streets remains to be seen. For the present, however, this walk will lead you by the huge, iron, covered market where the neighbors shop, and give you a vivid sense of how life was here a hundred years ago.

When you reach the C de l'Almirall Cervera, take a left and walk two blocks to the beach. This is the **Passeig Marítim;** head for the huge copper fish gleaming on the beach far ahead of you. You will walk along a seawall that looks down on the clean sand and palm trees of the **Platja Barceloneta** ("Barceloneta Beach"). As long as you see the green flag flying at one end of the beach or the other, it's perfectly safe to go in the water if you desire. There are people swimming here all year long, although a winter dip is more bravado than pleasure. There are lifeguards on duty during the summer months. Beneath the Passeig Marítim are a string of plain cafés that serve good food at extremely reasonable prices.

Walk by the Rebecca Horn sculpture on your right—four leaning iron-and-glass cubes stacked one on another. From here there is only beach—sand and palm trees—all the way down to sculptor Frank Gehry's remarkable huge copper fish in front of the Hotel Arts. Across from the beach is the Olympic Village, apartments constructed to house the entourage of people traveling with the athletes who came for the Olympics, later sold to Barcelonese. Beyond this is the Port Olímpic with its yacht basin and long row of restaurants offering everything from Tex-Mex to Japanese. The port's far boundary is a pier, the **Moll de Gregal,** with four fine continental-type restaurants on it, and beyond that yet another long stretch of beach, the Platja de Nova Icària.

The metro stop here is Ciutadella/Vila Olímpica on the yellow line (L-4). To get to the station, walk back to the Hotel Arts and head away from the water and the hotel, crossing the Ronda Litoral by the fountains and the roundabout to C de la Marina. Walk up one block to Av. Icària and turn left. The metro is two blocks down.

PARC DE LA CIUTADELLA ("THE CITADEL PARK")

This is the only real park in the old part of town, and is traditionall considered to be the lungs of city. It was built on the site of the citadel con structed in 1718 to house soldiers loyal to the Bourbon government in Madrid. For Catalans, it was a symbol of the Bourbon occupation, and roundly detested. Originally, it was a vast pentagonal tract of 270 acres. To turn it into a fortress for Felipe V's army, some 1,200 houses were razed practically destroying the maritime quarter of Ribera. When Barcelonet was constructed some 50 years later, it was supposedly to house member of families displaced by the Citadel.

In 1869, following the Revolution of 1868, the land was turned over to the city for use as a park. The people of Barcelona were eager to erase th military citadel, with its training grounds and huge barracks. The govern ment in Madrid agreed that 150 acres would be used to construct a park and 120 acres to build private housing, the sale of which would defray th expense of the park. A contest was held to determine the design for the new park. The winner was an architect named Josep Fontseré i Mestres, who assembled a design team. Included was a young Antoni Gaudí, only 21 year old and fresh out of architecture school, still years away from assuming hi place as the chief representative of the modernist movement. The park is a horseshoe within a horseshoe, featuring gravel walkways, museums, a zoo and two large, beautiful, iron horticultural buildings. The most amazing construction within the park, however, is the Cascade, an immense allegor ical fountain that is shocking in its first impression of oversize ugliness, bu is at the same time a fountain of astonishing proportions. Among its ele ments are griffins spouting water, river gods, Neptune, Leda, and Amphritrite, and a clothed Venus standing on a shell. The other body o water in the park is a small lake in its center, which can be navigated in rented rowboats.

What role the young Gaudí may have had in the fountain's construction or in that of the cast-iron entranceways to the park, is unknown, but if the Ciu tadella did not give him the opportunity to express himself, it helped a neo phyte architect make a living and keep body and soul together for a while.

Another eye-catcher in the Ciutadella is a sculpture of a young woman with a parasol done by Joan Roig i Soler. Other sculptures that draw com ment are a large cat and a life-sized woolly mammoth. Also remarkable are the two horticultural buildings—the *Hivernacle* ("Winter Garden") and the *Umbracle* ("Shade House"), which stand beside the Passeig de Picasso. The Hivernacle is a great glass-framed greenhouse. The Umbracle is also cas iron, but with its roof open to the air.

The Ciutadella is home to three museums. There is the **Museu d'Art Modern** ("Museum of Modern Art") (in the Plaça d'Armes, Tel. 319-5728, Fax 319

965), which houses a notable collection of Catalan artists from the 19th and 20th centuries, as well as collections of engraving and decorative arts from the region. Among the painters represented are Marià Fortuny, Santiago Rusinyol, Ramón Casas, Miguel Utrillo Canals, Pau Gargallo, and Isidre Nonell. Closed Tuesdays, open all other days 9 A.M.-9 P.M. Admission charge of $3.

The **Museu de Geologia** ("Geology Museum") (Tel. 319-6895, Fax 319-6312) is actually Barcelona's oldest existing museum, and it features a large mineral collection and paleontology exhibits, as well as the natural science collection bequeathed to the city by Francesc Martorell. Closed Mondays, open other days 10 A.M.-2 P.M. Admission charge of about $2.50.

The **Museu de Zoologia** ("Zoology Museum") (Tel. 319-6950, Fax 310-6999) is in an extraordinary neo-gothic building designed in 1888 for Josep Domenech i Muntaner for the Universal Exhibition of 1888, a world's fair that was held in the park. In those days it was a café/restaurant, but it currently houses zoological collections. It is closed Mondays, open all other days 10 A.M.-2 P.M.There is an admission charge of about $2.50.

Last, and perhaps least, in the Ciutadella is the **Barcelona Zoo** (Tel. 309-2500). It is an aging facility, drab and not particularly interesting except for one thing. The world's only albino gorilla—*Copito de Nieva* ("Snowflake")—has been in residence here since 1969. Currently in his forties, he's getting toward old age by gorilla standards and is not likely to be around all that much longer. Open daily 10 A.M.-6 P.M., March, Oct.; 10 A.M.-7 P.M., April, Sept.; 9:30 A.M.-7:30 P.M. , May-August; and 10 A.M.-5 P.M., Nov.-Feb. Admission charge of about $6.

5. Sports

The water is safe for swimming and fishing can be done from the long rock jetties that stretch out into the sea. If windsurfing is your thing, during the summer the beaches host a number of kiosks where they rent windsurf boards to those who want them. In addition to the possibility of sports on the sea, you can rent a bike or in-line skates from a number of kiosks at the Port Olímpic.

For those who prefer to do their swimming in a pool rather than the sea—which is a particularly good idea if the season isn't summer—there's the covered pool just along the beach beyond Barceloneta, the **Piscine Marítim.** It's open all year, 7 A.M.-9 P.M. Mon.-Fri., Sat. and holidays 8 A.M.-2:30 P.M., closed on Sunday. It costs 350 ptas. to use the pool, and a bathing cap is mandatory.

6. Shopping

The three square blocks behind the Set Portes restaurant, across from the post office, are the outlet for cheap electronic goods. They are sold in

one shop after another, along with watches, alarm clocks, and luggage. I
you want a calculator or an answering machine, this is a good place to loo}
first. It has the feel of West 14th Street in New York, where a lot of brand
name knock-offs are mixed in among the real things. You can save money
on some items here, but be careful to thoroughly inspect what you're buy
ing.

7. Nightlife and Entertainment

Planet Hollywood (C de la Marina, 19-21, Tel. 221-1111). If you've beer
in one anywhere in the world, you know what to expect: a movie-star deco:
with actual props that were used in famous movies and a lot of Hollywood
exotica. Offering a reasonably priced menu featuring California cuisine, the
place really gets going later in the evening when a young, hip crowd arrives
It's located right behind the Hotel Arts and the bar is open until 3 A.M. o1
weekends. The restaurant serves until 1 A.M. every night, and does not take
reservations.

Luna Mora (19-21 C de la Marina, Tel. 221-6161). Opened in the last hal
of 1996, close to the Hotel Arts and Planet Hollywood, this has quickly
become an "in" place for a young monied set. It has curving lines on the
first floor, with a stage and fairly ample floor space, although it gets crowded
depending on who the band is. It's live music three nights a week. There i
also a second floor with a full bar where peole go to get a little more privacy
although the fine sound system is always turned up. It costs $15 at the door
and that buys you a drink. Open every night, 10:30 P.M.-5 A.M.

Distrito Maritimo (Passeig de Colon). This is a modern bar on the Mol
de la Fusta with an ample outdoor terrace. On the weekends, after mid
night, it fills up with a young crowd who want to hear head-thumping
techno music on the high-quality sound system. Open until 3 A.M.

Polyester. Currently the in place to be among those in their twenties who
like to dress weirdly and throw themselves around a dance floor to a techno
beat, this club with two huge cement dance floors is located in a vast base
ment of the Estació de França. There is also a smaller lounge area where
lighter disco music is played and which is usually also jam-packed. The place
stays open until 6 A.M. on the weekends. The entrance is from the parking
lot beside the train station.

7

The Eixample

1. Orientation

In the mid-1800s, the city fathers decided to tear down the walls that had contained Barcelona to create more living space above the Plaça Catalunya. The project of designing the city's new configuration was awarded to Ildefons Cerdà i Sunyer, a great admirer of Manhattan's orderly streets. He created a 576-block grid of wide streets which currently connect the old city to the neighborhood of Gràcia, once a small town outside the city's walls.

The **Passeig de Gràcia** is the wide boulevard that runs from the Plaça de Catalunya to the Av. Diagonal, and also divides the Eixample between left (facing up, away from the sea) all the way to the Plaça d'Espanya; and right, stretching over to the Plaça Glòries. In addition to its pleasing order, its chamfered intersections, and its various "pocket parks," the Eixample is a pleasure to walk through because many of its buildings were constructed during the heyday of modernism by the movement's foremost architects at the turn of the last century. Almost any street in the Eixample contains a building that will stop you in your tracks with a beauty that is rarely encountered in other cities.

The Eixample offers travelers everything they require: fine restaurants, hotels, bars and cafés, cinemas, theaters, churches, and plenty of

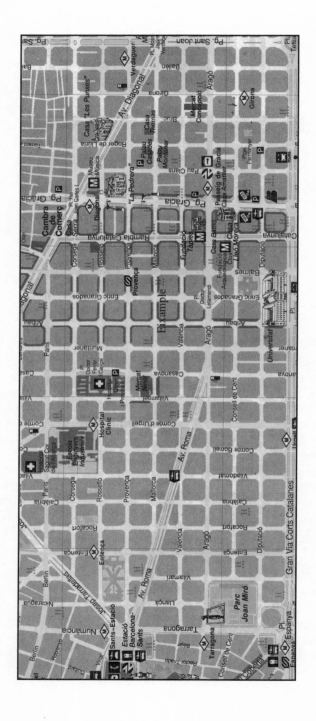

shopping. In addition, walking through the district's many residential streets is the best way to get a feel for what daily life is like for middle-class Barcelonese. This is the heart of residential Barcelona. If you have some time to fill while you're in the city, you can always take a metro, bus, or taxi to the Eixample and just start walking. You're bound to be rewarded.

2. The Hotel Scene

Claris★★★★ (150 C de Pau Claris, Tel. 800-888-4747, 487-6262; Fax 215-7970). In the 19th century, this was the Verduna Palace—and it looks it from the regal outside. The inside has been redone with marble and teak. The hotel's owner has what is reportedly Spain's best collection of Egyptian art, and some of it can be seen in the gallery on the second floor. There are 124 rooms, an outdoor swimming pool, and a sauna. Business conveniences. $250-$270, single; $285-$310, double. Breakfast buffet included.

The Palace★★★★★ (668 Gran Via de les Corts Catalanes, Tel. 318-5200, Fax 317-3640). Built as the elegant Ritz Hotel in 1919, it changed ownership in 1996 and is now the Palace. It has been refurbished a number of times since it opened in 1919, but it has lost none of its aristocratic clientele or atmosphere. There are 161 high-ceilinged rooms. The service is what you would expect from the most expensive hotel in the city. Located at the center of town, at the edge of both the old city and the Eixample. There is an excellent restaurant on the premises, and at 4 P.M. each day there is a tea service available in the indoor garden. $350, single; $380, double. Breakfast buffet included. Business conveniences.

Avenida Palace★★★★ (605 Gran Via de les Corts Catalanes, Tel. 301-9600, Fax 318-1234).This is a quiet, tasteful, richly appointed hotel with 159 rooms at the bottom of the Eixample. There is a gym and a sauna. While there is no private parking, spaces near the hotel are usually available, according to the staff, which is comprised of a particularly helpful group of individuals. Business conveniences. $165, single; $185-$200, double. Breakfast included.

Calderón★★★★ (26 Rambla de Catalunya, Tel. 301-0000, Fax 317-3157). A popular destination for business travelers, this hotel is centrally located and has 260 comfortable rooms. There is a a a restaurant in the hotel, as well as a rooftop swimming pool and a sauna. The staff is long accustomed to helping with the needs of people in town for business reasons. Business conveniences. $175-$190, single; $190-$210, double. Breakfast buffet included.

Condes de Barcelona★★★★ (75 Passeig de Gràcia, Tel. 484-8600, Fax 488-0614). This hotel is built around a narrow modernista building done by the architect Josep Vilaseca i Casanova in 1904. It has a total of 183 rooms here and in its sister hotel across the street. The rooms are comfortable and the staff is attentive. The hotel has a good restaurant, the Brasserie Condal, and enjoys a central location in the middle of the Eixample. Business conveniences. $135-$150, single; $150-$275, double. Breakfast buffet included.

Dante★★★ (181 C de Mallorca, Tel. 323-2254, Fax 323-7472). In a residential neighborhood of the Eixample and within a few blocks of everything, this is a popular choice among European business travelers. It is a delightful address from which to watch middle-class Barcelonese going about their daily lives. The 81 rooms have all the amenities. $145, single; $165, double. Breakfast buffet included. Business conveniences.

Majestic★★★ (70 Passeig de Gràcia, Tel. 488-1717, Fax 488-1880; in the U.S. call 800-332-4872). A favorite of frequent travelers to Barcelona, it has 335 rooms that offer all that could be expected, as well as English-language movies. There is a good restaurant. The staff is highly competent. It is in the middle of the Eixample, across the Passeig de Gràcia from the Comtes de Barcelona. $115, single; $130, double. Breakfast buffet included. Business conveniences.

Astoria★★★ (203 C París, Tel. 209-8311, Fax 203-3008). High up in the middle of the Eixample, a block below Av. Diagonal, this hotel offers 117 comfortable rooms in a convenient location. The staff is courteous and helpful. There is a restaurant and bar on the premises. There is no parking, although there are pay lots nearby, and occasionally a space on the street. $100, single; $125, double. Breakfast buffet included. Business conveniences.

Balmes★★★ (216 C de Mallorca, Tel. 451-1914, Fax 451-0049). Located in a wonderful section of the Eixample, on the corner of the C de Mallorca and the C Balmes, a block away from the Rambla Catalunya, this hotel was built in 1990 and is modern and fully equipped. The bathrooms are ample and there is a lovely garden and outdoor swimming pool. There is also a restaurant on the premises. Business conveniences. $125, single; $140 double. Breakfast buffet.

Condestable★★★ (1 Rda. Universitat, Tel. 318-6268, Fax 318-6268) is a modest but basically comfortable hotel across in a central location across the street from the university. It has 50 plain rooms that have ample bathrooms, air conditioning, and satellite TV. $55, single; $75, double. Breakfast buffet not included.

Taber★★★ (256 C Aragò, Tel. 487-3887, Fax 488-1350). Located just off the Rambla Catalunya with its upscale shops and cafés, this hotel has 91 fully equipped rooms with ample bathrooms and a comfortable lobby. $85, single; $100, double. Breakfast buffet included. Business conveniences.

3. Restaurants and Cafés

One delightful feature of spring, summer, and fall is that a number of the cafés along the Rambla Catalunya move tables and chairs out into the middle of the Rambla, underneath beach umbrellas. This is a very pleasant place to take a little liquid refreshment, day or night, with an endlessly entertaining parade of passersby. There is a **Farggi's** and a **Haägen Daz,** both of which have outdoor cafés and serve a variety of scrumptious ice cream dishes and drinks. There is also the **Forn de Sant Jaume,** just above C de Aragon on the Rambla, with a long line of tables and chairs outside. It is famous for its remarkable array of pastries. As with any café table, once you have ordered and consumed you are under no obligation to vacate the table until you are good and ready to do so. If you wish to relax and watch the passing crowd, do so to your heart's content.

Beltxenea (275 C de Mallorca, Tel. 215-3024). With an anteroom that looks like a living room from the past century, this restaurant in the middle of the Eixample offers Basque cooking in a lovely setting. On warm evenings, eat outside on the graveled patio behind the restaurant, surrounded by the backs of classic Eixample apartment buildings. Be aware that this is an expensive restaurant. Fish in spicy sauce is a specialty, but there is a wide range of tasty Basque dishes. The best ones are from the sea. Closed Saturday lunch and Sundays. Reservations necessary.

La Cerveceria Catalana (Right off the Rambla Catalunya at 236 C de Mallorca, Tel. 216-0368) is a bar/restaurant specializing in tapas. On one side as you walk in is a glass case on the bar full of a wide variety of non-seafood tapas. On the other side is the seafood. You can point to what you want and find a table in the back and a waiter will bring it, or eat at the bar. It's a great place to go, either for a snack or to make a meal out of the dozens of choices available. Each of these small plates of food is reasonably priced, but if you sample a lot you might work your bill up into the medium-price range. Usually crowded. No reservations.

Citrus Restaurantus (on the corner of Passeig de Gràcia and Consell de Cent at 44 Passeig de Gràcia, Tel. 487-8123). This is a delightful second-floor place in the middle of the Eixample (there's an elevator for older or disabled folks) for either lunch or dinner with an open, airy design. It opened in 1996 and proved immediately popular. Try to get one of a number of tables that look out on the Passeig de Gràcia. The menu is innovative and moderately priced, and the service is impeccable. For a first course the *Delícies de carbassó amb formatge de cabra i oregna* ("zucchini with goat cheese and oregano") comes highly recommended. For a second course try the *Ossobuco de vedella amb bolets de temporada* ("veal marrow with mushrooms of the season"). Reservations recommended. Open 1-4:30 P.M. and 8 P.M.-1 A.M.

Tragaluz (5 Passeig Concepció, Tel. 487-0196). Located in a beautiful passageway off the Passeig de Gràcia, close to Gaudí's La Pedrera, this expensive restaurant has a lovely, light and airy, wood and glass decor. Upstairs, it serves a creative cuisine based on Mediterranean flavors and the foods that are available in the market, depending on the season. Downstairs, there is an elegant Japanese tapas bar. Reservations necessary. Open daily 12:30-4:30 P.M. and 8 P.M.-midnight.

Casa Dario (256 Consell de Cent, Tel. 453-3135). In the heart of the Eixample, this medium-priced restaurant has been here more than a quarter century, serving a traditional Galician cuisine from the west coast of Spain. Among the house specialties are crepes with a sea urchin filling or cod in the Galician style. Reservations recommended. Closed Sundays. Open 1-4 P.M. and 8 P.M.-midnight.

Internet Café (656 Gran Via de les Corts Catalanes, Tel. 412-1915: the Internet bar upstairs; 302-1154: the bar and restaurant downstairs). The first restaurant/café in Barcelona to offer computer terminals and Internet connections to its clients, it is located at the bottom of the Eixample along the Gran Via. There are all the usual offerings of a bar and restaurant, in addition to an upstairs where for 600 ptas. per half-hour you can sit down and sign on. It's open 10 A.M.-midnight Mon.-Fri., 10 A.M.-2 A.M. on Fri. and Sat., and 5 P.M.-11 P.M. Sun.

Yu (204 C de Valencia, Tel. 451-9446). This Japanese restaurant is located in a narrow space in the Eixample, arranged in elegant simplicity. The food is traditional Japanese cuisine, with fresh ingredients prepared with a sure hand. An excellent Japanese restaurant with a more reasonably priced menu than its sister restaurant, **Yamidori,** around the corner on C Aribau. You can sit at the long curving bar and watch the chef make sushi from the tuna he buys each morning at the nearby covered Ninot market. The sushi and sashimi are both excellent, as is the *Yu maki,* a roll of rice around avocado and raw fish. The *gyoza* (large Japanese ravioli) are particularly tasty. Reservations are recommended. Open Mon.-Sat. 7 P.M.-12:30 A.M.

Mordisco (265 C de Rosselló on the corner of Passeig de Gràcia, Tel. 218-3314). This place has an artistic atmosphere that brings in a hip crowd of designers, models, and avant-garde types. The medium-priced selection is a combination of Catalan and French, with everything from fanciful salads to their interpretation of a hamburger. There are painting and sculpture exhibits and the walls are adorned with the work of Xavier Mariscal, who designed Barcelona's Olympic logo. Open every day but Sunday until 1 A.M. Reservations necessary.

Sahib (137 C de Entenza, Tel. 226-7225). There are not many Indian restaurants in Barcelona, but if you crave a taste of India you can find a good one in this restaurant located three blocks from the Sants train station. Offering a traditional Indian menu, its specialties are lamb dishes, any one of which is an excellent choice. Reservations are recommended. Closed Sundays. Open Mon.-Sat. 8 P.M.-midnight.

L'Hostal de Rita (279 C Aragó, Tel. 487-2376). A block and a half north of Passeig de Gràcia, this new, comfortable restaurant with its clean lines and good lighting serves up a well-prepared and tasty Catalan cuisine. They have a menu in English. The *souquet,* a hearty fish soup, is particularly recommended. Be prepared to wait 10-15 minutes in line. They don't take reservations and it's a popular place. It's worth the wait.

Rio Azul (92 C de Balmes, Tel. 215-9333). Chinese food in Barcelona tends to be about 30 years behind Chinese food in the States, with chow meins and chop sueys still dominating menus. Not so at this one, where there is a reasonably priced selection of excellent Mandarin cuisine specializing in Peking duck and seafood dishes. Reservations recommended. Open 1-4 P.M. and 8 P.M.-midnight.

Velódromo (213 C de Muntaner, Tel. 430-5198). Only a block below the Av. Diagonal, this is a big vault of a café/bar built in the early 1930s, with five billiard tables at the back and long leather sofas to sit on. It has a fine feeling to it, everything a roomy relaxed café should be. They serve tapas and bocadillos and it's open Mon.-Sat., 6 A.M.-3 A.M.

Vida Sana (603 Gran Via de les Corts Catalanes, Tel. 301-0376). The name of the place means "healthy life" and is appropriate for one of the scarce vegetarian restaurants in this carnivorous city. When you go in you pass through a health food store in the front (where you can also get sandwiches and meals to take out) and pass into the restaurant. The menu is moderately priced and creative, and the fresh, flavorful food is worth a try. Particularly good are the onion soup as a first course, followed by the moussaka. No reservations.

Laie (5 C de Pau Claris,Tel. 302-7310). This is a combination bookstore/café/restaurant that does an excellent job fulfilling each of these functions in its central location just below the Eixample and the Gran Via. The bookstore downstairs has an ample section of new books in English, and the café upstairs has plenty of daily papers, including the *International Herald Tribune,* available to those having a coffee or pastry. At lunchtime, the restaurant features a moderately priced buffet selection for the first course offering a number of tasty dishes that change each day, as well as an ample selection of scrumptious desserts. At night, diners order from a slightly more expensive menu featuring tasteful Mediterranean cuisine. No reservations. Closed Sundays.

Happy Books (286 C de Provença, Tel. 487-3001). A bookstore with primarily Spanish and Catalan books, but the café in its central open courtyard is a lovely place to take a cup of something regardless of the language you speak. There is a limited, minimal food menu, but it's a good place to come for an after-lunch cup of coffee. You can enter the bookstore and continue through it until you reach the courtyard with its tables. Open Mon.-Sat. 9:30 A.M.-9 P.M.

4. Sightseeing

RAMBLA DE CATALUNYA AND PASSEIG DE GRÀCIA

Beginning at the Plaça de Catalunya, a good way to see the heart of the Eixample is to walk up either the Rambla Catalunya or the Passeig de Gràcia and down the other. Let's begin with the Passeig. It is lined with upscale apartment buildings, boutiques, fancy shops, banks, offices, and cinemas. The tile mosaic benches and the wrought iron street lights along it were designed by Gaudí. This is one of the centers of Barcelona's economy, and executives mingle with tourists. An office address on the Passeig de Gràcia is about as good as it gets in Barcelona.

The street had its beginnings half a century before the rest of the Eixample was even conceived, as an extension of the line of La Rambla to connect Barcelona with the village of Gràcia. It was a start-and-stop kind of construction, depending on the state of public finances, but by the mid-1830s, it was in place—although as little more than a road between two towns through open countryside. Eventually, the Passeig became a favorite place for Barcelonese to walk and ride outside the dense streets of the city, and gradually the well-to-do began building along it. When the time came to design the Eixample, its principal street was already in place.

By the late 1800s, the street was *the* place to live for high society. In a pleasant coincidence, it was also the heyday of the modernist movement in architecture. A rare combination of circumstances: a flourishing architecture and a public with plenty of money to hire the architects, combined with newly created urban space in which they could work. Work they did. The Passeig presents some of the gems of the modernist movement.

The stretch of the Passeig between Gran Via and the C de Consell de Cent presents an array of heavy buildings, perfect in style for the large-scale business operations that now are headquartered there. Between Consell de Cent and C de Aragó, on the left-hand side going up, is the single block known as the *mansana de la discòrdia,* a block that is one of the architectural treasures of Europe. It contains three buildings, each built in the first decade of the 1900s by one of the three greatest modernist architects. *Mansana* means "apple" in Catalan, but also a "city block," so this translates as the "block of discord," said to refer to the difference in styles of the trio of modernists.

At 35 Passeig de Gràcia is the **Casa Lleó-Morera,** which was built in 1905 and designed by Lluís Domènech i Muntaner. The house has stone balconies carved to resemble flowers and winged lions extending from the walls. From across the street you can see the ventilator on top: in typical, whimsical, Modernist fashion that took the mundane and made it fantastic, this apparatus looks like an odd bonnet beribboned with green, pink, and yellow.

At 41 Passeig de Gràcia is the **Casa Amatller,** designed by Josep Puig i Cadalfach and completed in 1900. Note its Flemish-style stepped gable featuring animals sculpted in stone. Next door at 43 Passeig de Gràcia is the Casa Batlló, which was the total renovation of an existing building done by Antoni Gaudí between 1904-06. It is a wonderful example of the modernist master's mind at work. With its curving balconies, the whole building seems to be of something more human than stone, infused with a sense of ancient forms made new again. Its sensuous shape argues for a different concept of how a building can occupy space.

None of the three buildings in the mansana de la discòrdia is open to the public, yet one hardly need enter them to appreciate the departure modernism represented from the architecture that had preceded it. Don't be self-conscious about standing on the sidewalk outside these buildings, or on the sidewalk across the Passeig de Gràcia from them, and craning your neck upwards or staring. You are likely to be in company, as people can almost always be found along this stretch doing just these things day or night. At night, the Casa Batlló is illuminated and takes on an even stronger presence.

Only a few blocks up and across the boulevard, at 91 Passeig de Gràcia, is the **Casa Milà** (Tel. 487-3613), an apartment house considered to be one of the first-rank Gaudí creations. It was commissioned by a wealthy developer, Pere Milà i Camps, who decided to celebrate his marriage by building the most outstanding building on the Passeig de Gràcia. He hired Gaudí in 1906 and told him to have at it. The great architect did so, and the result was a building finished in 1910 that is among the most outstanding of modernist works.

Generally referred to as *La Pedrera* ("The Stone Quarry"), this remarkable, sinuous, curving structure is supported entirely by parabolic arches and columns; the stone walls play no role in its continuing to stand upright. It is reputed to have not a single true straight line or right angle on the premises. It was neglected for a number of years during the Franco dictatorship—neither Gaudí's fierce Catalan patriotism nor his sense of play and whimsy sat well with the dictator. The building is currently owned by La Caixa de Catalunya, Spain's largest savings bank, and they have done a laudable job of restoring it to its former bizarre elegance. Its lovely curves and soft lines are topped by a rooftop terrace, with some remarkable chimnies and ventilators. There are tours conducted Tue.-Sat., at 10 A.M., 11 A.M., noon, and 1 P.M., that enable visitors to see the central part of the building and the roof. However, all the apartments are still in private hands and not open. The tours are free, but they only accomodate 30 people at a time so you may want to turn up early.

One block to your left is another lovely boulevard, the **Rambla de**

Catalunya, which parallels the Passeig de Gràcia. It, too, features toney shops, nice restaurants, cinemas, and upscale apartment buildings. It also has a broad pedestrian rambla running down its center, lined with benches on which the weary may rest for free. In addition, a number of cafés have comfortable chairs and tables on the rambla, and it's a lovely place to stop for a little something on a nice day. With its combination of refinement and accessibility, the Rambla de Catalunya is a marvelous and restful street, which includes a number of simply breathtaking apartment buildings that have balconies of tall, stained-glass windows jutting out over the sidewalk.

At 57-59 Rambla de Catalunya is the **Museu Egipcï** ("Egyptian Museum") (Tel. 488-0188) with three floors of relatively small exhibition space housing some 300 pieces from ancient Egypt. The museum is administered by a private foundation, and its exhibitions are well-displayed, with a high standard of quality dominating the collection. Admission is about $3. Open seven days a week from 10 A.M.-2 P.M. and 4-8 P.M.

The part of the Eixample between C de Muntaner and C Roger de Flor, which encompasses Passeig de Gràcia and the Ramblya Catalunya, is currently referred to as the **Quadrat d'Or** ("Golden Square") of modernist architecture. There are plaques on over 100 buildings identifying their architects and the year of their completion. Among the most interesting are the **BD Design Store** at 291-93 C de Mallorca, in an edifice which was built by Lluis Domenech i Muntaner, and two buildings on Av. Diagonal done by Josep Puig i Cadalfach, one at 416-420, the **Casa Terrades,** a bizarre building with pointed towers, so that many Barcelonese call it the "house of spikes." At 373 Av. Diagonal is the **Casa Vidal Quadras,** which currently houses the **Museu de la Música** ("Museum of Music") (Tel. 416-1157). The museum features a collection of musical instruments beginning as far back as the 16th century. There are also exotic instruments from Asia and Latin America. General admission of about $4. Closed Mondays. Open Tue.-Sun. 10 A.M.-2 P.M.

Another remarkable example of Domenech i Muntaner's work is the **Fundació Antoni Tàpies** (255 C Aragó, Tel. 487-0315), which was one of his earlier buildings, completed in 1881. The building became the fundació in 1989 to house the work of Catalunya's most well-known contemporary artist, who people generally love or absolutely cannot relate to. It's an easy place to find because Tàpies put a sculpture of his own on the roof, a huge, tangled mass of wire called "Cloud and Chair." The foundation also has temporary exhibits by other artists. Open Tues.-Sun. 11 A.M.-8 P.M. There is an admission of approximately $4.

LA SAGRADA FAMILIA

On the right side of the Eixample are three other modernist works that one should visit. The first is to be seen even if you see nothing else and is, of course, **El Templo Expiatorio de la Sagrada Familia** ("the Expiatory Temple of the Sacred Family"), which Gaudí worked on constantly for 25 years before his death and which some believe will never be finished, although construction continues apace. It has eight astounding spires in place and no roof. It is an odd, whimsical, and remarkable cathedral that is Barcelona's most emblematic sight. Gaudí was anything but a whimsical person; he was a conservative Catholic and a Catalan nationalist. But in his work he gave free rein to his imagination, making liberal and amazing use of the forms and movement of nature in his designs, and he imparted to his buildings a life of their own.

In addition to being a pure delight to view from outside on the sidewalk at ground level, or from the back across the small park behind the cathedral, you can pay an admission charge of less than five dollars and go inside the cathedral grounds, where for another dollar or so you can ride the elevator up the inside of one of the spires. You can save the money and walk up the twisting narrow stone steps, but they stretch 450 feet into the sky and you had better be in shape to do it. A better idea is to ride the elevator up and walk back down, stopping along the way to enjoy the remarkable and slightly dizzying views offered from high above the city.

The plans that Gaudí left behind for the cathedral were sketchy at best, and many argue that it should be left uncompleted, rather than pour public and private funds into a project that will result in something far removed from what its creator envisioned. There are two sides to this question; the blocky, chunky sculptures at the front representing the Ascension, executed by Catalan sculptor Josep Subirachs, can be seen as an argument for leaving well enough alone. They are out of harmony with the rest of the cathedral and have none of the flowing grace of Gaudí's work. They are a distraction at best.

On the other hand, the six musicians sculpted over the back portal by Japanese sculptor Etsuro Sotoo integrate beautifully with Gaudí's work, complementing and joining it, and demonstrating, perhaps, that the project might be successfully carried to completion if approached with the proper sensibilities. Sotoo came from Japan to visit Barcelona over two decades ago, fell in love with Gaudí's work, and stayed, eventually becoming one of the two sculptors entrusted with the work. He represents an interesting phenomenon, which is the deep response felt by many Japanese to Gaudí's work. A substantial amount of the private funds to continue work on the cathedral have come from Japan over the years, and Japanese tourists flock to the site.

Regardless of which side of the question you are on, work on the cathedral is continuing. For all the changes in the place since Gaudí died, however, the additions merely distract in a minor fashion from the genius of the cathedral as it went up under the master's hand. Neither bad sculpture nor straight lines can dim the brillance of Gaudí's creation. To reach the Sagrada Familia, take the purple line (L-2) or the blue line (L-5) of the metro to the Sagrada Familia stop.

The other most remarkable modernist work on the right side of the Eixample is the **Hospital de la Santa Creu i Sant Pau** ("Hospital of the Holy Cross and Saint Paul"). There are not many cities in the world in which a hospital is on the short list of things to be seen, but this one certainly qualifies. This remarkable complex of buildings was designed in 1902 by Lluis Domenech i Muntaner to be the city's new hospital. The medieval hospital, Antic Hospital de la Santa Creu, was badly outdated, and the city desperately needed a better medical facility. In keeping with his character, Domenech i Muntaner did not design a standard hospital. In fact, he designed something that had never been done before. He decided to create a hospital that would facilitate the healing process on fronts other than the strictly medical. He reasoned that patients who have access to beauty, fresh air, and a healthful environment would heal faster. The hospital, which covers 360 acres—nine square blocks of prime Eixample real estate—was filled with details large and small that would facilitate a patient's healing. Colorful mosaic work, flowing forms, domes, trees, and the sense of a peaceful garden within the walls of the hospital are all designed to promote recovery at every turn. As of this writing it was still a working hospital, although there is frequently talk of moving it to somewhere more modern and contemporary. Visitors are free to wander through its grounds.

Another modernist building you may want to visit is currently serving as the **Centre Cultural de La Fundació Caixa de Pensions** ("Cultural Center of the La Caixa Savings Bank Foundation") (108 Passeig de Sant Joan, Tel. 458-8907). Located not far from the Sagrada Familia cathedral, just above Plaça Tetuan, the Foundation mounts revolving exhibits of art and photography, usually of high quality. Information on what is currently being shown there can be found in the Cartelera of the daily newspapers. It is located in a striking modernista building, thought by many to be one of architect Josep Puig i Cadalfach's finest. There are also occasional chamber music concerts in the enclosed garden, as well as a café and bookstore. Open Tue.-Sat. 11 A.M.-8 P.M. and Sundays 11 A.M.-3 P.M. Closed Mondays and holidays.

5. Sports

Bullfighting is not considered a sport by most Spaniards so much as an art (in the newspapers, reviews of bullfights run alongside theatre, concert, and film reviews and not on the sports pages). Just beyond the Sagrada Familia, at 749 Gran Via de les Corts Catalanes—just a little beyond the actual boundaries of the Eixample—is the city's only surviving bullring. There used to be another, all the way across the Eixample in the Plaça d'Espanya, but it has been closed for many years now. The impressive circular structure still stands—despite a number of ideas proposed over the years—empty.

Catalans are not as wild about bullfighting as the rest of Spain, particularly the southern half of the country. While good crowds turn up here most Sundays for the 5:30 P.M. event during the bullfight season from March to Sept., they are mostly people from other parts of the country or international tourists. In fact, in 1995, there were over 6,000 officially registered complaints calling for a ban on bullfighting and over 80 percent of them came from Catalunya. This also means that many of the best matadors prefer to perform somewhere else, where their work will be more appreciated and rewarded.

Nevertheless, if you're not going to get to a part of Spain with a higher concentration of bullfight aficionados, it is worth taking in one here if you want to get a sense of what it's all about. This is also the site of the **Museu Taurí** ("Museum of Bullfighting") (749 Gran Via de les Corts Catalanes, Tel. 245-5803). It is just what the name says, with a collection featuring the stuffed heads of famous bulls, posters of corridas, and "suits of lights," the clothes worn by matadors. There are also a number of photographs. There's an admission charge of about $2.50. Open April 1-Sept. 1, 10:30 A.M.-1 P.M. and 4:30-8 P.M.

For the swimmer, during summer, half a block above the Sagrada Familia is a pair of outdoor pools, called **Piscine Municipal Claror** (333 C de Sardenya, Tel. 207-0640). They are open June 15-Sept. 15 and cost about $6 to swim for a day.

6. Shopping

Those who enjoy **auctions** will want to check with the Eixample's auction houses to see when their monthly auction (*subasta,* in Spanish) is scheduled. These include **Balcli's,** 227 C del Roselló (Tel. 217-5607); **Sotheby's,** 2 Passeig Domingo (Tel. 487-5272); **Brok,** 167 C de Pau Claris (Tel. 215-5028); and **Subarna,** 257 Provença (Tel. 215-6518).

Adolfo Dominguez (89 Passeig de Gràcia, Tel. 215-1339). This store near the top of the Eixample has an international reputation for its products, designed by the most well-known of Spain's designers. Conservative and of the highest quality, these are clothes that will not go out of date. The store has two floors, one for each sex.

Alataïr (71 C de Balmes, Tel. 454-2966) is a large bookstore in the center of the Eixample devoted to travel and anthropology, with travel guides in a wide variety of languages for just about any place you can think of and many that you can't. It also has a nice section of photography books, and is altogether an excellent place to while away an hour easily on a rainy day and an indispensable location if you're looking for a travel guide. It is one of the most attractive bookstores in the city. It is loaded with English-language travel guides from the standard tourist guides to the more exotic items in travel literature, as well as a considerable selection of travel writing and anthropology in English and an excellent array of recorded world music.

BD Ediciones de Diseño (291-293 C de Mallorca, Tel. 458-6909). This is the showroom of one of the top interior design firms in the country. A sizeable part of what is happening in interior design in Spain can be gleaned from a trip here to see their furniture and accessories.

Bulevard Rosa (55 Passeig de Gràcia, Tel. 309-0650). Called a galeria, this was the equivalent of Barcelona's first mall: a collection of more than 100 shops selling designer clothes, bags, shoes, and a wide variety of other goods. For a while after it opened in the 1980s, this was the bee's knees in Barcelona's shopping, but other more upscale and American-type malls have recently opened and taken away a good deal of clientele. It's open Mon.-Sat. 10:30 A.M.-8:30 P.M.

Camper (249 C de València, Tel. 215-6390) is a store in the Eixample featuring women's shoes and handbags, popular among the go-fast designer bar crowd.

Crisol (34 de Consell de Cent, Tel. 215-3121). This is a well-stocked bookshop with a somewhat limited selection of best sellers and detective novels in English, as well as a wide range of magazines. A busy, cheerful store.

E. Furest sells top-of-the-line menswear, offering both traditional and contemporary clothes designers from around the world. Three locations: at 3 Av. Pau Casals (Tel. 203-4204); 12 Passeig de Gràcia (Tel. 301-2000); and 468 Av. Diagonal (Tel. 218-2665).

Groc. Tony Miró is a Catalan fashion designer whose clothes are proudly worn by many of Barcelona's young and chic. His prices are high but his relaxed and alluring designs are comfortable and graceful. This store sells men's clothing, women's evening and daywear, shoes, and Chelo Sastre jewelry. Made-to-order is available. Two Eixample locations: 100 Rambla de Catalunya (Tel. 215-0180) and 385 C de Muntaner (Tel. 202-3077).

Joaquin Berao (277 C del Rosselló, Tel. 218-6187) offers contemporary jewelry by a leading avant garde jewelry designer. The store is a jewel in itself.

Laie (85 C de Pau Claris, Tel. 318-1739). Its second-floor restaurant and café have their own listing elsewhere in this guide, but the bookstore on the ground floor also deserves mention, as it is one of the best in the city, featuring a substantial (if somewhat expensive) selection of English-language books, magazines, and newspapers.

Loewe (35 Passeig de Gràcia, Tel. 216-0400) is the city's best-known name for fine leather goods. Art critic Robert Hughes has called for a boycott of Loewe's because of the way they modified the ground-floor facade of the beautiful modernist building, the Lleó Morera house designed by Lluis Domenech i Muntaner that they occupy. (They put in display windows.) Judging by the crowds often found shopping there, the critic's ire has not hurt business. There are two other locations, one specializing in menswear at 570 Av. Diagonal (Tel. 200-0920) and the other, in women's clothing at 8 C Johann Sebastian Bach (Tel. 202-3150).

Vinçon (96 Passeig de Gràcia, Tel. 215-6050). One of Barcelona's most famous stores, it offers design and home furnishings, gadgets and gee-gaws, kitchenware, fabrics, furniture, food, design books, and a wide array of other interesting products. There is a lovely terrace upstairs and an ongoing series of art exhibits.

Zara (67 Rambla Catalunya, Tel. 487-0818). This store is a branch of a chain found in Paris, Lisbon, and New York that features well-made clothes for men, women, and children at more reasonable prices than most places here. They often have a limited number of sizes of any given item, but if you find something that fits, it's likely to be of good cut and quality. Open 10 A.M.-2 P.M. and 4 P.M.-8 P.M.

Despite the fact that there are plenty of music aficionados of all kinds in this city, there is a surprising dearth of places to buy recorded music. There are only two really big music stores. One is **Virgen Music** (Tel. 412-4477) at the corner of the Passeig de Gràcia and Gran Via. This is the megastore in town and a good place to look for most any kind of music, from classical to Catalan folk and everything in between. It has two floors of CDs and a knowledgeable staff, if you can get their attention in all the confusion. It's open 10 A.M.-9:30 P.M. Mon.-Thur.; 10 A.M.-10:30 P.M. on Fri. and Sat.; closed on Sundays.

The other large recorded music store, which opened in 1995, is **Planet Music** (214 C de Mallorca, Tel. 451-4288), which is a much nice placer to shop than the warehouse ambience of Virgen. It's located in the heart of the Eixample and its sales staff is helpful and attentive. Although it is smaller than Virgen, it is widely praised for its selection of alternative rock, headbanger, jazz, and flamenco music. It's open 10 A.M.-9 P.M.

At the far right-hand side of the Eixample, in the Plaça de les Glòries, is the **Centre de les Glòries,** which houses nearly 100 stores. It's the equivalent of most malls in the States, with middle-class offerings, nothing too upscale, but solid, durable goods and representatives of some of Barcelona's most reputable retail companies. It is a nicely designed mall with a lot of outdoor space. The Plaça de les Glòries is a working-class neighborhood that the city has been reclaiming. For a different style of shopping, this is also the longtime site of the Barcelona flea market, **Els Encants.** This market is on the far side of the plaça from the mall, offering a wide range of shopping styles for those who make the journey. It is open Mon, Wed., Fri., and Sat. until 7 P.M. The flea market mixes antiques, second-hand goods, and just about every other thing you can imagine. There are some bargains mixed in with the junk, but look carefully before you pay. Shopping in the Plaça de les Glòries can be an all-day exercise if you do a slow tour of both the mall and the flea market. In case this happens to you, the restaurants around the flea market serve respectable, hearty meals at lunch for reasonable prices. Take the metro, the red line (L-1), to the stop called Glòries.

7. Nightlife and Entertainment

Daily Telegraph (139 C de Pau Claris, Tel. 215-1779). One of a wave of recently popular British and Irish bars where they serve a wide variety of excellent beers and whiskies, have dart boards and Anglo decor, and often, like this one, a large television screen for sports programs.

Ideal (89 C d'Aribau, Tel. 453-1028). This is an adult cocktail bar with red plush comfortable chairs, sofas, and a subdued atmosphere, modeled loosely after an English pub with hunt prints on the walls. They feature a wide selection of single malt scotches and mix a good *mojito*, the delicious Cuban specialty of rum, sugar, lime juice and mint, which was Hemingway's favorite drink. You are not likely to encounter many people here with nose-rings, and conversation or amorous exchanges are the norm with the music for background purposes only.

Nick Havana (208 C del Rosselló, Tel. 215-6591). One of the original designer bars, done in 1987 by Eduard Samsó, it features a trendy crowd of people drinking and getting to know one another in the midst of loud music and a high level of noise, although there is no room for dancing. There are a number of unusual features, however, including a bank of 30 television screens and a vending machine that sells paperback bestsellers.

Velvet (161 C de Balmes, Tel. 217-6714). One of the earlier designer bars in l'Eixample, the interior was done by Alfredo Arribas. It has loud music, trendy decor (including stools designed to snugly hug a person's derriere), and a party atmosphere, all crammed into a fairly small space. Open daily 7:30 P.M.-3 A.M.

Café de les Arts (234 C Valencia, Tel. 454-5838). A favorite among the younger yuppie set, the place is packed after midnight on the weekends. There's a large back room with a lot of space; nevertheless, it gets crowded as the nights wears on, particularly on a weekend. There's good music and wall-to-wall people, and if you want to see how young, middle-class Barcelonese like to relate on the weekends, stop in for a drink. It's open 6:30 P.M.-2 A.M. Mon.-Thur. and 6 P.M.-3 A.M. Fri. and Sat.

Satanassa Antro Bar (27 C Aribau, Tel. 451-0052). The reference to Satan in the name and the sardonic drawing above the door set the tone for this bar favored by a young set. Inside there's scarcely room to breathe as the pulsating lights and the music keep people up and flinging themselves about wildly. The line of people under 25 waiting to get in the door on a weekend night will deter all but the most determined. It's open 10:30 P.M.-3 A.M. Sun.-Thur. and 10:30 P.M.-3:30 A.M. Fri. and Sat.

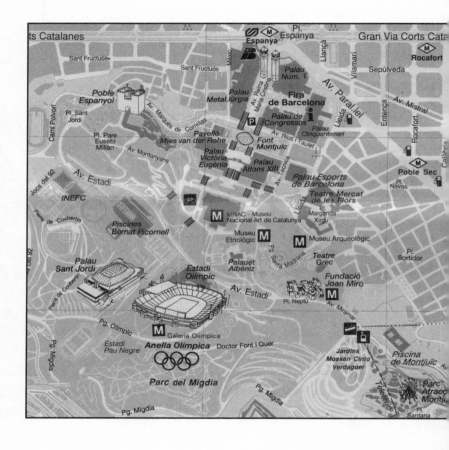

8

Montjuïc

1. Orientation

In the Middle Ages, the Jews of the city were buried on Montjuïc. Most people believe that is where the hill got its name: Mount of the Jews. The old Jewish cemetery has been destroyed, and some of its headstones are said to have been used by Gaudí in the building of La Sagrada Familia. Now it is the Catholics who bury their dead on Montjuïc, and their city of the dead with its many fancy crypts enjoys a remarkable view of the Mediterranean.

Barcelona nestles up against Montjuïc. The high hill has always been important to the city's well-being. The hill borders the southern side of the city where it meets the sea, and is most easily reached from the Plaça d'Espanya. At the far end of the Av. Maria Cristina, which runs into the plaça, is the National Palace. From the avenida, Montjuïc is accessible by car, bus, or escalator.

Much of Montjuïc is as it has always been: hilly, undeveloped green space, where you can walk for a long time without seeing many other people, and from which there are innumerable lovely views of the city and the sea stretching away behind it. City historians believe that Montjuïc was a population center for the pre-Romans who lived here. During Roman times it was *Mons Jovis,* the "Mountain of Jupiter," and it was populated (some hold that the name Montjuïc thereby derives from this, rather than from the Jews).

Despite its role as an ancient dwelling place, the hill's use for the living sinc
the Middle Ages has been somewhat sporadic and sparse. A huge castl
and fortified complex was built in the 1600s, and Montjuïc has always serve
as a cemetery, but otherwise it has not been of major importance to thos
living in Barcelona. In this century, Montjuïc has undergone two grea
growth spurts, each coming as a result of international events—the 192
International Exposition and the 1992 Summer Olympics.

The first large-scale development around Montjuïc in this century cam
as a result of the 1929 International Exposition, when some 15 palaces wer
built, along with a stadium high up on the hill, and the Poble Espanyo
down at the bottom. In the following years, little additional use was mad
of the area. Many of the attractions created for the run-up to 1929 wer
allowed to deteriorate, receiving little use. Generally, the citizens c
Barcelona made as little use of their untrammeled green space as they di
of their seaside. Then came the Olympics, more than 60 years later, and
new wave of development rejuvenated the area, including the constructio
of the Fira de Barcelona, the city's primary convention center site.

2. The Hotel Scene

Barcelona Plaza★★★★ (6-8 Plaça d'Espanya, Tel. 426-2600, Fax 42€
0400). This hotel, with 338 rooms, is in a functional, chunky-looking buil⊂
ing on the Plaça d'Espanya. Although it's a little ways from the city's cente
it is perfectly located for people attending fairs, congresses, and conver
tions at the trade center across the plaça. It has a nice health club and
helpful staff who speak good English. Business conveniences. $142, singl€
$160, double. Breakfast buffet included only on weekends; it's another $1
a day to park your car.

3. Restaurants and Cafés

Rias de Galicia (7 C de Lérida, Tel. 424-8152). This restaurant, close t
the convention center in the Plaça d'Espanya, offers a fine example of Gal
cian cuisine (food from the west coast of Spain). Something from the se
is the thing to order here, be it *mariscos* ("seafood") or *pescado* ("fish")
because nowhere are freshness and flavor paid more respect than in Galici
Reservations recommended.

Fundació Joan Miró. Not only does the Joan Miró Foundation house
spectacular collection of Miró's work and that of other artists, but it has a
air-conditioned bar and restaurant that is open from noon to 6 P.M. It is
good place to eat after seeing the collection, particularly if it's summe
and you're not quite ready to be back out in the hot sunshine.

1. Sightseeing

Take a metro or bus to Plaça d'Espanya and go to the Av. Maria Cristina. This street is easy to spot because it has the great, looming **Palau Nacional** ("National Palace") at one end. Here, you can catch the number 61 bus that will bring you up Montjuïc, past the Olympic stadium, and as far around as the Fundació Miró. The climb up Montjuïc loops off to the right where Av. Maria Cristina ends, and becomes the Av. del Marquès de Camillas. Shortly, it passes the **Poble Espanyol** ("Spanish Village") (located at Av. del Marquès de Comillas, Tel. 325-7866) on the left. There is also a bus, a red double-decker English affair that will carry you straight from the Plaça d'Espanya to the Poble Espanyol.

Originally built for the 1929 International Exposition, the grounds of the Poble Espanyol cover some five acres and are devoted to showcasing the architecture and crafts of Spain's various regions. The streets and squares of the village are lined with examples of traditional architecture from regions as distinct as Andalusia and Galicia. The village has 35 shops offering representative crafts in ceramic, glass, metal, and leather from the various regions, as well as places to eat and drink. Quality of both crafts and food ranges from good to mediocre, and prices are generally quite a bit higher than you will find elsewhere for comparable purchases in the city. Nevertheless, for those with limited time who would like to get a glimpse of how Spain sees itself, this can be a fun stop. There is also a museum here, the **Museu d'Arts, Indústries i Tradicions Populars** ("Museum of Popular Art, Industry, and Tradition") (Av. Marquès de Comillas, Tel. 423-6954, Fax 423-0196). It includes Spanish handicrafts and rural implements, tools, artisanal crafts, religious objects, toys, and clothes, as well as an entirely reconstructed antique pharmacy. Free to those who have paid the admission price for the Poble. Call for hours, although it is generally open the same hours as the Poble Espanyol. Admission to the Poble is about $5. It is open 9 A.M.-8 P.M. Mon.; 9 A.M.-2 A.M., Tue., Wed., Sun.; 9 A.M.-3 A.M. Thur.; and 9 A.M.-6 A.M Fri. and Sat.

Just beyond the Poble Espanyol is the **Mies van der Rohe Pavillion** on the left. Built in 1986, it is a replica of the architect's building for Germany at the 1929 exhibition. It has been widely reproduced in office waiting rooms around the globe. When van der Rohe built it, he was considered to have made an important architectural statement with its clean lines, light, stone, and glass. Immediately following the exposition, the building was demolished. More than fifty years later the replica was built. It is open 8 A.M.-8 P.M. daily and is free.

Carry on up and around the hill; on the right-hand side is a plaza and a place to look out across the plain and wetland toward where the river Llobregat empties into the sea. The Llobregat, which runs near the airport, has recently recovered its capacity to support the most elemental riverine flora and fauna, following a spell during which it was incapable of supporting any life at all. The overlook is called the **Mirador del Llobregat.**

On your left you'll see the sign for the **Palau Nacional** and the **Jardines de Montjuïc.** The gigantic, neo-classical palau was built for the 1929 Exposition by modernist Luis Puig i Cadalfach. In 1934 it was dedicated as the **Museu Nacional d'Art de Catalunya** ("National Museum of Catalan Art") (on the Mirador del Palau, Tel. 423-7199, Fax 325-5773) to house a collection which had been held, since its beginning in 1891, in a building in the Ciutadella Park. During the Olympic years it was remodeled by the Italian architect Gae Aulenti, who also worked for the city of Paris and turned an abandoned train station there into the Musée d'Orsay. The job she did in Barcelona was hailed by many when the Palau reopened in 1995 and decried by others.

Whatever one's opinion of Aulenti's work, there is no doubt that the museum holds one of Europe's finest collection of early medieval paintings, the most outstanding of which are a series of Romanesque frescoes removed by Italian craftsmen from the walls of a number of small churches in the Pyrenees and pre-Pyrenees. Among the most notable pieces are the frescoes from the apse and paintings from the walls of Santa Maria de Taüll, consecrated in 1123. These make up one of the most complete and best-preserved specimens in the museum. The apse is reigned over by the Virgin Mary. The murals include scenes of the Magi following the guiding star to Bethlehem, as well as the confrontation between David and Goliath. The frescoes from Sant Joan de Boi are from the 12th century, including a number of interesting representations of fantastic animals and a scene with three jugglers. Other extremely well-conserved paintings come from Sant Climent de Taüll and Sant Pere de Sorpe.

Other outstanding features of the museum are the Romanesque and Gothic altarpieces and sculptures. Also in the museum are works by Tintoretto and El Greco. Outside the museum is the first of the available great views of the city from Montjuïc. Closed Mondays. Open Thursdays 10 A.M.-9 P.M.; Tues., Wed., Fri., and Sat. 10 A.M.-7 P.M.; and Sundays 10 A.M.-2:30 P.M.

From here, the Av. del Marquès de Comillas continues to climb the hill. On your right, the so-called **Anillo Olimpíco** ("Olympic Ring") begins with a lovely classical Greek building by one of Barcelona's most famous architects, Ricard Bofill. This was built for the 1992 Olympics when it was used as a venue for the wrestling events. It subsequently has been incorporated into the university system as the school of physical education.

This building is followed by the **Piscines Bernat Picornell** (the "Bernat Picornell swimming pools"), where the Olympic swimming and diving competitions were held. It has one Olympic-sized indoor pool, as well as two outdoor pools, and it is their elevation under the Montjuïc sky that provided so many memorable television pictures of the diving competitions, with the divers standing on the boards in front of the backdrop of the city. The pools are open to the public (See "Sports," below).

The next thing on the right is the restful botanical garden, with benches for those looking for a little rest in the shade. Beyond it is the **Palau Sant Jordi,** an indoor stadium that served as the site of the gymnastics events during the Olympics and is often used now for the very big-name music shows that can hope to pack well over 20,000 people into a building. It has a mushroom-shaped dome. The building and the plaza it sits in were designed by the noted Japanese architect, Arata Isozaki. As soon as all these things were completed prior to the Olympic games, the citizens of Barcelona began returning in great numbers to Montjuïc and putting them to use. The plaza in front of the palau is a particularly popular place for local families to come after a late midday meal on Sundays. Children run around chasing each other or kicking soccer balls while adults make themselves comfortable on the grass or the benches and pass the time, often sipping and nibbling a little something. Next to the palau is the 60,000-seat stadium, which was extensively renovated for the 1992 games. Nevertheless, its heavy, imposing architecture still bears some of the hallmarks of a Europe at the end of the 1920s, leaning toward a big, imposing, facist architecture enamored of the monumental. The stadium is open to the public seven days a week from 10 A.M.-8 P.M. and whenever there is a sporting event there. The Palau Sant Jordi is open only for events, and the plaza in front of it is opened to the public on Saturdays and Sundays from noon to 8 P.M.

Carrying on around Montjuïc, the road changes names to the Av. Miramar, and you'll shortly pass by the **Fundació Joan Miró** ("Joan Miró Foundation") (Plaça Neptu, Parc de Monjuïc, Tel. 329-1908, Fax 329-8609) on the left. One of Catalunya's best two artists of the century (Salvador Dalí is the other), Miró donated his collection of both his own work and that of other artists to the Fundació, as well as enough money to hire José Lluís Sert to build the foundation's home above the *Jardin Amargós* ("Amargós Garden") on Montjuïc. Sert was an associate of the great French architect Le Corbusier. He lived in the States in exile during the Franco years and taught at Harvard. The building is a work of art, ample and comfortable with lots of light and a number of windows giving onto open space and the city below. Among the fine pieces in the building is Alexander Calder's Mercury Fountain. Miró's own choices show his work as it evolved from its beginnings. Outside the front door is a large, impressive sculpture by Eduardo Chillida. The Foundation is a fitting memorial to the great Catalan artist who died in 1983 and lies buried in the nearby Montjuïc cemetery. In addition to a large number of Miró's works, including some of his best sculptures and paintings, the Foundation hosts traveling exhibitions. There is also a research library, an art bookstore, and a snack bar. Open Tue.-Sat. 11 A.M.-7 P.M. (Thursdays until 9:30 P.M.). There is an admission charge of about $5. Closed Mondays and holidays.

A little further along on your right is the teleferic station where you can get a cable car that will carry you further up the hillside to the Montjuïc attractions park and on to the **Museu Militar** ("Military Museum"), which features a collection of antique and modern weaponry, models of forts and castles, lead soldiers, and present-day military uniforms. Open Tue.-Sun. 9:30 A.M.-1:30 P.M. and 3:30-7:30 P.M. Located in Montjuïc Castle (Tel. 329-8613), which was built in 1640. It has a tragic history for Catalans, as it has been the site over the years of numerous executions. The most recent, in 1940, was of the last president of the Generalitat prior to Franco's taking of the city in 1939—Lluís Companys i Jover. Today, a stone marks the spot where he fell dead before the firing squad. Even if military museums are not your thing, this is a must because the grounds in front of the building offer a remarkable view of the edge of the city and the sea. Should you stay on the Av. Miramar, you can wind around and descend Montjuïc.

Also on Montjuïc is the **Museu Arqueològic** ("Archeological Museum") (Passeig de Santa Madrona, Tel. 423-2149, 423-5601; Fax 425-4244), a museum of general prehistory, featuring the colonization of Catalunya and the rest of the Iberian peninsula, with material from a variety of cultures including Talayot, Punic, Iberian, Greek, and Roman. There are also items from the Etruscans and the Visigoths, and from Catalunya's Middle Ages. Free on Sundays. Open Tue.-Sat. 9:30 A.M.-1:30 P.M. and 3:30-7 P.M., Sundays and holidays 10 A.M.-2 P.M. In the same park is the **Museu Etnològic** ("Ethnological Museum") (Tel. 424-6402, Fax 423-7364), which houses an extensive collection of ethnological items including ritual and religious art from New Guinea, Japan, Afghanistan, and Guatemala. Closed Mondays. Open Tuesdays and Thursdays 10 A.M.-7 P.M., all other days 10 A.M.-2 P.M.

5. Sports

Montjuïc offers the possibility of both spectator and participatory sports, including the **Piscines Municipals Bernat Picornell** (30-40 Av. de l'Estadi, Tel. 423-4041), which were built for the 1992 Olympics, close to the Olympic Stadium on Montjuïc, and are now open to the public. There is an admission fee of 1,000 ptas. and the pools are closed on Sundays. Its hours are 7 A.M.-10 P.M. Mon.-Fri.; 7 A.M.-9 P.M. Sat.; and 7:30 A.M.-2:30 P.M. Sunday.

The **Piscina Municipal Montjuïc** is another municipal pool with a great bird's eye view of the city. It is two outdoor pools, further down the mountain, but looking straight across to La Sagrada Familia. It costs 650 ptas. to use the pools. It's open June 1-Sept. 30, 10 A.M.-6 P.M. Mon.-Fri.; 10 A.M.-5 P.M. on Sat.; and 10 A.M.-2 P.M. on Sundays.

For those who prefer a spectator sport, there are home games of the **Barcelona Dragons,** the city's entry in the world league of American football. This is hardly professional pigskin as people know it stateside, more like a fairly good college team, but if you want to watch a football game on a nice day in the stadium where the Olympic track and field events were held, this is the place to do it. Next door in the palau is where **FC Barcelona,** the city's professional basketball team, plays. Again, it's not up to NBA standards, although the team always has a couple of Americans playing who are at that level. But it's hard fought, good basketball, and the home games are listed in the sports pages of the daily newpapers. Tickets can be bought from the large ticket kiosk on the corner of Gran Via and C Aribau, by the university, and at the stadium.

6. Shopping

Apart from the arts and crafts sites in the Poble Espanyol, the gift shop in the Fundacio Miró, and the souvenir T-shirts and caps in the kiosk inside the Olympic Stadium, Montjuïc offers little in the way of shopping.

7. Nightlife and Entertainment

The most notable nightspot here is the amazing **Las Torres d'Avila** (Av. del Marquès de Comillas, Tel. 424-9309). Located in the Poble Espanyol, this is a prime example of what Barcelonese mean when they refer to "designer" bars. This one was designed by Javier Mariscal, who created the logo for the Olympic Games in 1992, and Alfred Arribas. It occupies several levels of glass and steel staircases, with seven bars and a glass elevator to transport patrons between levels or up to the rooftop terrace with its huge moon. The place reportedly cost over $5 million to construct. Even the bathrooms are out of the ordinary with their sleek chrome fixtures and stark lighting. The sound system here is excellent, although there is no dancing. The price of the drinks starts at about $10.

La Discoteca del Poble Espanyol is designed for a younger, somewhat less affluent crowd and is known by its unofficial name, **On/Off.** Be forewarned: this is an after-hours club; that means things do not start getting underway here until about 6 A.M. on Saturday and Sunday mornings. The music is mostly techno, more people are high on Ecstasy than alcohol, and you can dance until 9 or 10 A.M. It's a spacious, ultramodern club with a good sound system.

9

The Zona Alta
(The Upper Zone)

1. Orientation

The "zona alta" refers to a number of neighborhoods that are spread across the upper part of the city, above the Av. Diagonal. Many people whose stays in Barcelona are brief do not find time to explore the higher parts of the city above the Av. Diagonal. If they do visit it's to see the Parc Güell or the Monestir Pedralbes, and that is the extent of it. There are numerous things worth seeing in this vast part of the city, although they tend to be spread out. It is in the upper reaches of Barcelona where the wealthy live, and there are numerous lovely buildings. The shopping in this area is on a level equal to that of the Eixample. There are also more parks above Diagonal than there are below, and a complete list in Catalan can be obtained from the lovely little book, *Parcs i Jardins de Barcelona*, available in the Palau Virreina for about $2.50. Despite the wide geographic area represented by the designation Above Diagonal, this section basically takes in places you might want to visit from the southern side represented by the Monestir de Pedralbes to Tibidabo, the Vall d'Hebron, and the Parc Güell toward the north.

2. The Hotel Scene

Barcelona Hilton★★★★★ (589 Av. Diagonal (08014), Tel. 419-2233, 800-

445- 8667; Fax 405-2573). Located on the upscale end of the Av. Diagonal, it has the modern architectural style for which the chain is known. There are 288 rooms, including some no-smoking rooms, some designed for disabled guests, and a pair of executive floors, one of which is reserved entirely for businesswomen. There is a formal restaurant and a café. Business conveniences. $250, single; $285, double. Breakfast buffet included.

Rey Juan Carlos I★★★★★ (661-667 Av. Diagonal (08028), Tel. 448-0808 Fax 448-0607). Also located on Av. Diagonal, not far beyond the Hilton, this hotel was opened in 1990 and named for the king of Spain. It is close to the university and the exclusive Pedralbes neighborhood. The hotel has three restaurants, one of which is Japanese. There is an outdoor swimming pool. The 375 rooms are large, modern, and comfortable. There is also a health club. Business conveniences. $260, single; $300, double. Breakfast buffet included.

Hotel Rekor'd★★★★ (352 C de Muntaner, Tel. 201-1953, Fax 414-5084) This small hotel has 15 large and comfortably furnished suites, each with a mini-office and all the comforts of any fine hotel. Located close to the Via Augusta, it is in the middle of the fancy commercial area above the Av. Diagonal, and is an excellent location for anyone here to do more business than sightseeing. Business conveniences. All rooms have two double beds. $120, single; $140, double. There is no breakfast.

Princess Sofia★★★★ (Plaça de Pius XII (08028), Tel. 330-7111, Fax 330-7621). A nice, less expensive alternative to the Hilton or the Rey Juan Carlos, this hotel is named after the queen of Spain. Out toward the toney Pedralbes district, it's everything you look for in an upscale big-city hotel with 511 modern rooms. It's on the Av. Diagonal and a couple of blocks from a branch of Barcelona's largest department store, El Cortes Inglés. A convention-oriented hotel, it also features an indoor swimming pool, fitness center, and sauna. Business conveniences. The rooms are ample and comfortable. $150-$175, single; $150-$200, double. Buffet breakfast included.

TRYP Presidente★★★★ (570 Av. Diagonal (08021), Tel. 200-2111, Fax 209-5106). Located in an upscale part of the city, this is a favorite among Europe's frequent travelers. It has 156 ample and comfortable rooms with all the amenities, and a staff that offers a high level of service. Business conveniences. $160, single; $190-$215, doubles. Breakfast buffet included.

Covadonga★★★ (596 Av. Diagonal, Tel. 209-5511, Fax 209-5833) is located only a stone's throw away from some elegant shopping. This hotel is part of the Best Western chain and offers 85 comfortable rooms with a pleasant and helpful staff. No parking. Business conveniences. $83, single; $120 double. Breakfast buffet included.

Gala Placida★★★ (112 Via Augusta (08006), Tel. 217-8200, Fax 217-8251) is a little far away from the city center, about 10 blocks above the Av

Diagonal. But it is right down the street from the Institute for North American Studies, which has a good library and many current periodicals from the States, including daily copies of the *International Herald Tribune*. It's in an upscale neighborhood and is an apartment/hotel complex with 31 rooms, each with sitting room, fireplace, dining area, and refrigerator. All the rooms are doubles; $80-$90. Breakfast included.

3. Restaurants and Cafés

Masía Can Borrell (Tel. 691-2904) is one of a number of old Catalan farmhouses in the Collserola hills that have been converted into restaurants. The food is inexpensive, substantial Catalan fare. Particularly good is the *conill a la brassa* ("grilled rabbit"), served with *all i oli*, which is a garlic and olive oil combination whipped until it has the consistency of mayonnaise. Many restaurants take shortcuts in the time-consuming preparation of this stupendous condiment, but not this place. On weekends, particularly on Sundays, it's extremely crowded, so call ahead and make reservations. There is not really a specific address for the place. Driving the main road of the Collserola, the Carretera de Cerdanyola, look for the sign between kilometer four and three on the Sant Cugat de Vallés side of the hills, then turn back toward the left and follow the dirt road for about a mile, until you come to a field surrounded by parked cars and the old farmhouse.

El Asador de Aranda. There are two of them and both of these expensive restaurants are located in luxuriously comfortable settings. They specialize in the cuisine of Castile, which includes grilled meats and sausages that are notably famous. The restaurant at 31 Av. Tibidabo (Tel. 417-0115), close by the Museu de la Ciència, is in a remarkable, palatial modernista building begun in 1903 by Joan Rubió i Bellvé. The second branch is at 94 C de Londres (Tel. 414-6790). Reservations are advised. Both restaurants are open 1-4 p.m. and 9 p.m.-midnight Mon-Sat., 1-4 p.m. on Sundays.

Neichel (16 bis. Av. Pedralbes, Tel. 203-8408) is a very expensive restaurant that prepares its exceptional continental-style dishes with Catalan ingredients. Luxurious and elegant, the menu may feature such all-star offerings as lobster salad garnished with quail eggs and truffle strips or filet of sea bass in cream of sea urchin. It has two Michelin stars and has been ranked among the 10 best restaurants in Spain. Reservations are necessary. Open Mon.-Fri., Saturdays for dinner and closed Sundays, holidays, and during the month of August.

Flash-Flash Tortilleria (Between the Av. Diagonal and the Travessera de Gràcia, close by the Via Augusta, at 25 C de la Granada del Penèdes, Tel. 237-0990). This moderately-priced restaurant specializes in *tortillas*, which is Spanish for "omelette." In addition to the classic Spanish omelette (eggs

and potatoes), there are over 100 other varieties on the menu. It opene
in 1970 with a success that has not diminished. No reservations accepted
Open daily noon-1:30 a.m.

Bar Mirablau (in the Plaça Funicular, Tel. 418-5879). This bar is locate
at the end of Av. Tibidabo where you get the funicular to take you to th
amusement park. It has huge windows and offers a spectacular view of th
city and the sea beyond from its perch. If the tables by the windows are occu
pied, there is also a terrace. It is a lovely place to have a glass of something
Open daily noon-3 a.m.

4. Sightseeing

MUSEU MONESTIR DE PEDRALBES

The **Monastery of Pedralbes** (9 C Baixada Monestir, Tel. 203-9282, Fa
203-9988) was founded in 1326 by Queen Elisenda de Montcada, the fourth
wife of Jaume II (*el Just*). After he died, she spent the last four decades of he
life living on the premises. The monastery has been designated a nationa
treasure, a monument of historic and artistic importance. Located consid
erably above Av. Diagonal, at the edge of the toney Pedralbes neighbor
hood, it features a two-level Gothic cloister with murals by Ferrer Bassa don
in 1343. The simplicity of its exterior walls and the harmony that their hor
izontal line evokes with the vertical bell tower were praised by as eminent ar
architect as the great Le Corbusier.

The monastery has a museum that contains numerous fine examples o
medieval art. In addition, in 1992, a part of the remarkable Thyssen-Borne
misza collection—most of which is housed in Madrid—was put on exhibi
tion at the monastery, where it will remain at least until the year 2000. Thes
are 72 paintings and 8 sculptures, including some marvelous pieces from
Italy's baroque period in the 1700s. These are housed in their own museum
within-a-museum at the monastery. The monastery's museum costs about $
to enter; for another couple of dollars you get a ticket to see the Thysser
collection as well. The monastery is open Tue.-Sun. 10 A.M.-2 P.M. and Sat. 1
A.M.-5 P.M.; closed on Mondays.

PALAU DE PEDRALBES

Located far out the Av. Diagonal, on the right-hand side going away from
the city, is this lovely Italianate palace built in 1929 as a royal residence. I
later served as a guesthouse for visiting dignitaries. The gardens feature
small fountain done by Gaudí. The palace is currently the site of the **Muse**
de Ceràmica ("Ceramic Museum") (686 Av. Diagonal, Tel. 280-1621), which
houses what has been called one of the most important collections o

medieval ceramics in Europe. There is a collection of glazed Spanish pot-tery beginning in the 12th century and extending through the 19th, demonstrating both changing styles and technical innovations. There are also rooms where the contemporary ceramics of such artists as Miró and Picasso are exhibited. The **Museu d'Arts Decoratives** ("Museum of Decorative Arts") is part of the Ceramics Museum and features a collection of pocket watches dating from the mid-16th century, as well as an outstanding collection of Spanish glass. Open Tue.-Sun. 10 A.M.-2 P.M.

PARC GÜELL

Located above the Travessera de Dalt, this public park (Tel. 424-3809) was originally conceived of as a site for an upscale housing development on a hillside above the city, sponsored by Gaudí's patron Eusebi Güell. The idea was that Gaudí would design the main park area and other architects would provide plans for the homes. However, it turned out that few among Barcelona's upper classes were eager to live in a place dominated by Gaudí's spectacularly unusual forms, and the housing part of the project was abandoned for lack of response.

The city eventually took over the park in 1922. It is one of the most visited sites in Barcelona. Displaying Gaudí's love and reverence for natural forms, the park takes full advantage of the hillside on which it is built, its paths and columns following the sinuous lines of the ground. At its center is a large esplanade with a mosaic-covered bench, the stone of which seems to ebb and flow in a style contrary to the properties of rock and cement. The entrance to the park is remarkable for its playful gatehouse and huge mosaic dragon, which is almost as emblematic of the city as the spires of La Sagrada Familia.

Inside the park is also the house in which Gaudí lived from 1906 until his death, designed by his disciple, Francesc Berenguer, which has become the **Casa-Museu Gaudí,** open Mon.-Fri. 10 A.M.- 2 P.M. and 4-6 P.M. (Tel. 284-6446). The park is open daily 10 A.M.-6 P.M., Nov.-Feb.; 10 A.M.-7 P.M., March and Oct.; 10 A.M.-8 P.M., Sept. and April; and 10 A.M.-9 P.M. May-Aug.

TIBIDABO

This is the city's highest peak of the Serra de Collserola along the northern side of the city. It features an amusement park, charming for its old-fashioned rides and attractions, with an admission price of 600 ptas. The views from Tibidabo are outstanding. On a clear day one looks across the city, from one end to the other. Even better is the vista from the glass elevator that goes up the outside of the 800-foot-high communications tower, designed by British architect Norman Foster and built in 1992. It stands astride Tibidabo and for 300 ptas. you can ride up to its observation tower.

The best way to get to Tibidabo is to take the train (the FF.CC. de la Generalit) to the tramvia blau, which takes you up the Av. Tibidabo. At the end of the line you can get a funicular to carry you the rest of the way up.

Before taking the funicular, you might want to get off and explore the **Museu de la Ciència** ("Museum of Science") (55 C Teodor Roviralta, Tel. 212-6050, Fax 418-8751). Founded by the Caixa savings banks, this is a lively and interesting museum dedicated to bringing science to the public. In addition to the permanent exhibits of interesting optical effects, mechanics, computers, and a planetarium, there are revolving exhibits that are often quite interesting. There is also a separate hands-on exhibit for children three to seven, with an additional admission charge. The museum costs 450 ptas. and the kids' part an extra 300 ptas. It's well worth it. Open Tue.-Sun. 10 A.M.-8 P.M.

COLLSEROLA

The hills above Barcelona are a nice place to spend an hour or two hiking. There are many footpaths through the woods and a number of old Catalan farmhouses, called *masías,* which have been converted into restaurants offering tasty Catalan dishes at reasonable prices. A pleasant Sunday afternoon can be spent hiking through the hills until you have worked up an appetite, then repairing to one of these restaurants to spend a couple of hours at the table under the old wooden beams that cross the high ceilings.

There are public buses that go up to and along the Collserola, primarily bus number A-7, but then you will still have a little hike ahead of you to reach a restaurant. Well worth it, but easier if you have a car. Be forewarned if you go tramping through the more rugged parts of the Collserola: the wild boar in these hills, called *jabalí* here, are so numerous that a hunting season has been opened to thin their numbers. An angry boar is not to be taken lightly, but they are generally shy. If they hear you coming they will run rather than fight.

5. Sports

The part of the city above Diagonal offers considerable pleasure both in terms of participatory and spectator sports. To begin with, the Av. Diagonal comes highly recommended for those who like to ride bikes. A lane has been marked off in the pedestrian boulevard that runs alongside Diagonal from the Plaça Francesc Macia almost down to the Plaça de les Glòries Catalanes.

Above its starting point in the Pl. Francesc Macia, Diagonal is bordered along one side by a wide, tree-shaded pedestrian esplanade, which runs out to the Palau de Pedralbes. Bikes are not only provided lanes here, but are rented by the hour (600 ptas. per hour) in the Plaça Reina Maria

Cristina, out Diagonal, across from El Corte Inglés. While Barcelona's pedestrians are not always disposed to easily cede walkable pavement to oncoming cyclists, dealing with them is much less stressful than being out in vehicular traffic, and the bicycle route does virtually cross the city.

There are other things to do. Just a few blocks out from the Plaça Francesc Macia, above Diagonal, is the **Parc Piscines i Esports** (25-27 Ganduxer, Tel. 201-9321), with an outdoor pool. Open June-September, 9 a.m.-5 p.m., it costs 650 ptas. for a day's use.

On the opposite side of town, beyond Tibidabo, is the **Vall d'Hebron** neighborhood nestled up against the foot of the Collserola. It's the location of a couple of best bets for the sports-minded. The **Piscina Lars Mundet** ("Lars Mundet Swimming Pool") (171 Passeig Vall d'Hebron, Tel. 428-2750) is on the right outside the metro stop for Vall d'Hebron on L-4, the green line. There is one pool indoors and two outdoors. Cost for use is 750 ptas. per day. The pools are closed Sundays and open Mon.-Fri. 8 A.M.-9:30 p.m., Saturdays 8 A.M.-2 P.M.

But aquatic diversion is not all that the Vall d'Hebron has to offer. It was the sight of the Olympic tennis competition, which featured some of the world's greatest players. Now these same courts are open to the general public. If you want to play on a clay surface it will set you back 2,000 ptas. an hour; on a hard surface the cost goes down to 1,500 ptas.

6. Shopping

L'Illa (557 Av. Diagonal, Tel. 444-0000). It's a big mall on three levels that occupies three city blocks along the Av. Diagonal, out toward Pedralbes. It's chock-full of both nationally and internationally recognized stores like Benetton, Marks & Spencer, Zara, Hermès, Maica di Magni, and on and on for a total of some 78 commercial sites—which include, of course, places to drink and eat. There's a parking garage below the mall. Stores are open 10 A.M.-9 P.M., Mon.-Sat.; closed Sundays.

Enric Majoral (slightly above Av. Diagonal at 19 C de Laforja, Tel. 238-0752) offers lovely, handmade jewelry made primarily of silver and oxidized bronze. Majoral is one of the city's most interesting jewelry designers.

Indigo (432 Av. Diagonal, Tel. 416-1980). There are lots of places in the city to buy imports from India and Indonesia, but this is one of the consistently better ones. It has everything from cloth to furniture, clothes to jewelry, all of good quality. Located on Diagonal just past C de Pau Claris, it's open weekdays 10 a.m.-1:30 p.m. and 4:30-8 p.m., and Saturdays 10:30 a.m.-2 p.m.

Margarita Nuez (3 C de Josep Bertrand, Tel. 200-8400). Fine lines of women's clothing in a variety of beautiful fabrics are what's in stock at this shop just above the Turo Park and the Plaça Francesc Macia.

Sara Navarro (598 Av. Diagonal, Tel. 209- 3336). This shop features elegant, fashionable footwear and some lovely leather goods, including jackets and handbags.

Tema (10 C Ferran Agulló , Tel. 201-3998) offers the finest in high fashion by such internationally known Spanish designers as Manuel Piña and Jorge Gonsalves, who is said to be one of Queen Sofia's favorites. Also by Turo Park and above the Plaça Francesc Macia.

7. Nightlife and Entertainment

El Patio Andaluz (242 C d'Aribau, Tel. 209-3378). A nightclub located a block above the Av. Diagonal, it's a good bet for those who want a dose of flamenco. Shows here do begin as early as 10 p.m., but featured performers do not usually come on until after midnight.

La Boite Mas i Mas (477 Av. Diagonal, Tel. 419-5950). Just behind the Plaça Francesc Macia, it holds a long bar and a warm room that make for good listening. Jazz and blues all week, from 10:30 p.m. to 5 a.m. There's a 1,500-pta. cover, and that buys your first drink.

La Cova del Drac (33 C Vallmajor, Tel. 200-7032). The city's oldest jazz club, located above the Via Augusta, it features live jazz six nights a week in a plush lounge setting. The cover charge is 1,500 ptas. and that entitles you to a drink.

La Luz de Gaz (246 C de Muntaner, Tel. 209-7711) is a genuine cabaret with comfortable seating and a well-lit stage, located just above Av. Diagonal. The admission is about $18 at the door and can be well worth it, depending on who is performing. Recently, the club has been featuring the city's best salsa musicians on the weekends, and there is a small space for dancing. So if Latin music is your thing, check out the Cartelera in the newspaper to see who is playing here. Closed Mondays. Open 8 P.M.-1 A.M. Sun. and Tues.-Thur., and 8 P.M.-3 A.M. Fri. and Sat.

Up and Down (179 C de Numancia, Tel. 204- 8809). This discotheque and restaurant is a perennial favorite among those in Barcelona who want to see and be seen, from sports stars to visiting jet-setters. The disco is downstairs with a 2,500 pta. cover charge. There is a restaurant and somewhat more sedate bar upstairs.

Otto Zutz (15 C Lincoln, Tel. 238-0722). A big box, this large club has three levels on which to drink, each with its own bar where you can stand looking over the railing to the dance floor below. There is frequently live music and the sound system is good. There's a lively, young, and monied crowd. Located one block off Balmes, considerably above Diagonal, close to the Via Augusta, and not far below Plaça Molino. It doesn't open until midnight, and closes around 5 a.m. on Mon.-Thur., 6 A.M. Fri. and Sat. There's a 2,000-pta. cover charge at the door.

10

Day Trips into Catalunya

The autonomous region of Catalunya covers some 12,370 square miles and is divided into four provinces: Barcelona, Tarragona, Llerida, and Girona (these last two are Lérida and Gerona, respectively, in Castilian). It includes a wide range of geographies from the over-developed beaches of the Costa Brava to the scantily populated, rugged gorges of the Pyrenees mountains.

Most of the sites listed below can be reached by public transportation, but some are best seen with a car. Where you can take a bus, call the **Estació de Nord** for information at 80 C de Ali-bei (Tel. 265-6508); for train information, call the **Estació de Sants** at Plaça Països Catalans, s/n (Tel. 319-6416). Your hotel may have bus and train timetables, or you can check with the **tourist office** in the Plaça de Catalunya (Tel. 304-3135, Fax 304-3155).

The places listed here are perhaps the most noteworthy to visit, but there is also great fun to be had and many things to see for those who have the time and means to rent a car and spend a few days wandering around. Catalunya is full of small villages on the same ground they have occupied since the Middle Ages. It is also full of Romanesque churches, archeological marvels, and small fishing fleets anchored in protected harbors where the bright lights of a seafood restaurant by the docks gleam at night.

SITGES

Another tourist destination, **Sitges** is almost as well known in its own right as Barcelona. In fact, numerous people choose to base themselves in Sitges and come into Barcelona to visit, rather than the other way around. Sitges' main attraction is that it's a small, lovely town by the sea, within a half-hour of Barcelona by car or train. Despite its village size, Sitges is an extremely cosmopolitan locale—partly because it is the number-one place for gay tourists in Europe.

Tolerant, relaxed, and pleasant, it's a good place to go for a day and an evening. During the day there are a number of attractive beaches and a lovely seafront promenade, lined with cafés and bars. At night there are a remarkable number of bars and clubs going full-blast that cater to both gay and straight clienteles. Trains leave from the Sants station or the Passeig de Gràcia approximately on the half-hour, but be aware that the last train back from Sitges to Barcelona leaves at 10:27 P.M.

There is a wide selection of hotels for those who want to stay in Sitges, unless you are looking in August when a hotel room in Sitges can be extremely hard to find. The **Hotel Terramar**★★★★ (Paseo Maritimo, 08870, Tel. 894-0050, Fax 894-5604), right on the beach, has 209 air-conditioned rooms, with a swimming pool if you want to stay out of the salt water, tennis courts, and an 18-hole golf course beside the hotel. $125, single; $145, double. Breakfast included.

Another highly recommended seaside hotel is the elegant **San Sebastían Playa**★★★★ (53 Port Alegre, 08870, Tel. 894-8676, Fax 894-0430), with 51 comfortable double rooms beside the sea, a swimming pool, and a high level of service. All rooms are $150 with a buffet breakfast included.

There is also the **Hotel Subur**★★★ (Paseo de Ribera, s/n, 08870, Tel. 894-0066, Fax 894-6986), right in the middle of Sitges and some 250 yards from the beach. It has 95 recently renovated comfortable rooms, and a swimming pool, as well as a friendly, helpful staff. $80, single; $90, double. Breakfast buffet included.

For a memorable meal, try the seafood specialties at the relatively pricey (but well worth it) **Mare Nostrum** (60 Passeig de la Ribera, Tel. 894-3393). This place is also noted for its wine cellar. Reservations recommended. Closed Wednesdays and from Dec. 15 to Jan. 15.

Another fine place to go for fresh seafood dishes, including delicious thick fish soups, is **Fragata** (1 Passeig de la Ribera, Tel. 894-1086), which adds a terrific view across the sea from the top of a cliff to the attractions contained in its reasonably priced menu. Reservations recommended. Closed Thursdays.

In addition to the beaches, nudist and otherwise, there are some interesting things to enjoy in Sitges. One is the **Palau Maricel,** long maintained by the town as a conference center, but recently opened to the public. It's a prime example of modernist architecture, designed in 1910 for the American millionaire Charles Deering by painter Miguel Utrillo. It is only open to the public in the summer, when for an admission fee of about $6 you can take a leisurely tour, enjoy the beautiful views over the town and sea, and take a free glass of cava in the cloisters.

The second, and perhaps most notable, site is the **Museu Cau Ferrat** ("Iron Den Museum") (on the C Fonallar, Tel. 894-0364), which has one of Europe's best collections of wrought ironwork as well as a lovely collection of paintings including work by El Greco and Utrillo, and some Picasso sketches. Closed on Sunday afternoons and Mondays.

Close by is the **Museu Marciel de Mar** (Tel. 894-0364), which houses a relatively small, but nevertheless interesting collection of medieval art, sculpture, glass, and mosaics. It's open Tue.-Fri.

SANTA COLOMA DE CERVELLÓ

This remarkable village, some 20 minutes south of Barcelona by train, was designed by Gaudí under the patronage of Eusebi Güell to serve as a residential village for those who labored in Güell's textile factory in the same location.

The factory is currently an industrial park, and the houses are still occupied, frequently by descendants of the families who toiled for Güell. The homes are quite lovely and the entire village is built around a large open green with plenty of space.

Perhaps the most intriguing feature of the village is its church. At first glance it bears no resemblance to La Sagrada Familia. It is a low, squat building, set back in a wooded glen, with none of the sweeping lines of the cathedral. Yet closer inspection reveals many themes in common. The lines of the church are flowing and sinuous, in keeping with the natural world in which it is located. It is not so much imposed on the landscape around it as built into it. On a sunny day, the stained glass windows are beautiful. The stone of the church and the pine trees that surround it join together in an impressive harmony.

The trains (*Ferrocarils de la Generalitat de Catalunya*) that stop in Santa Coloma de Cervelló leave the Plaça d'Espanya at 15 and 45 minutes past the hour between 7 A.M. and 9:45 P.M. daily. From the train stop at Santa Coloma it's a three-minute walk along the side of the highway to the Colonia Güell. You can also drive there by taking the A-2 freeway and turning onto route N-340.

FIGUERES

This is an unremarkable Catalan town deep in the Empordà plain, a couple of hours north of Barcelona. What makes it worth visiting is the remarkable Salvador Dalí museum, the **Teatre-Museu Dalí** (28 C de Pojada Castell, Tel. 972-511-800), designed by the great surrealist master and every bit as weird and fabulous as his paintings. Dalí was born in 1904 in Figueres. He worked in the house that became the museum from 1974-1982, then remained bedridden there until his death in 1989. He was buried beneath a large glass dome in the museum's inner courtyard.

The museum is packed with some of Dalí's finest paintings and sculptures, and the building is a work of art unto itself. There is virtually no corner of the museum without its creative surprise. This is what Dalí wanted to leave behind him on his home turf, and fans of the painter will want to budget hours here.

The museum is the second most visited in Spain, after the Prado in Madrid, so you may want to schedule your stop there during lunch hours, when Spaniards will be eating. More than 300,000 people visited it in 1995. There is an admission charge of 400 ptas. and a gift shop with numerous reproductions of Dalí's work at a range of prices going from $10 to $100. From Oct. to June the museum is closed on Mondays and open other days 10:30 A.M.-5:15 P.M. From July to Sept. it is open seven days a week, 9 A.M.-7:15 P.M.

There are also some notable restaurants in Figueres. The restaurant in the **Hotel Ampurdan★★★** (Kilometer 763, Antigua Carretera de Francia, Tel. 972-500-562, Fax 972-509-358) is considered by many to be among the top-ranking restaurants in Spain. It serves classical Catalan dishes for reasonable prices, often using recipes that use meat and fruit together, such as the rabbit and prune terrine. What's more, if you want to stay overnight in Figueres, the restaurant is in a hotel of the same name with 42 simple but adequate air-conditioned rooms. $85, single; $100, double. Breakfast not included. The restaurant and hotel are open daily year-round. Reservations are necessary in the restaurant.

Another notable hotel/restaurant combination is the **Durán★★★** (5 C Lasauca, Tel. 972-501-250), a family-owned place in the center of Figueres' old town. The restaurant's reasonably priced fish and seafood dishes come well recommended. The restaurant is open every day, and reservations are advised. The hotel was opened in 1870, but its 65 rooms are modern and comfortable with air conditioning. $75, single; $90, double.

CADAQUÉS

This wonderful town on the coast is some 75 miles north of Barcelona. An hour's drive northeast of Figueres, it is where Dalí lived for much of his life. A beautiful whitewashed town, it was a quiet fishing village for many centuries, nestled along the coast in a natural harbor and cut off from the rest of the world by a high range of hills. During the summer it is an artist's colony and a popular tourist spot. The water is a crystalline turquoise and the swimming and snorkeling are excellent. Many families rent houses in Cadaqués by the week, and a favorite thing to do is gather mussels off the rocks for the evening meal.

There is also a hip, international nightlife and some exceptionally good restaurants. The six-mile drive across the hills from the main road to Cadaqués is full of switchbacks and hair-pin turns, and is best negotiated during the day. It's worth it, though, because the town is so lovely once you get there.

Among the hotels are the **Playa Sol★★★** (5 C Platja Pianch, Tel. 972-258-100, Fax 972-258-054), which has 50 modern and wholly adequate rooms overlooking the sea, and it has a swimming pool, tennis courts and a cafeteria. $80, single; $120, double. Breakfast buffet included. Closed Jan. 10-Feb. 28.

The **Rocamar★★★** (Virgen del Carmen s/n, Tel. 972-258-150, Fax 972-258-650) offers 70 comfortable and ample air-conditioned rooms right on the beach with tennis courts, sea-water swimming pool (heated for winter use), and a sauna. There is a restaurant in the hotel. Open all year. $100, single; $130, double. Breakfast buffet included.

A half-mile up the coast is a little cove called **Port Lligat,** where Dalí lived in a house that still stands down by the fishing boats, a house marked most prominently by two huge plaster eggs on the rooftop. Across the road there is a hotel, also named **Port Lligat★★** (Port Lligat s/n, Tel. 972-258-162, Fax 972-258-643), that offers guests some rooms with terrific views of the quiet cove, as well as a sun room from which you look down on Dalí's house. There are 30 rooms all told, with a swimming pool in summer and a restaurant. The rooms are simple, but adequate. It's closed on weekdays Nov.-March. $50, single; $65, double. Breakfast not included.

One restaurant of note (it has a Michelin star) is **La Galiota** (9 C Narcis Monturiol, Tel. 972-258-187), with reasonable prices and superb continental cuisine. Reservations recommended. Open only April 15-Sept. 15.

Another wonderful family-owned and -operated place to eat is **Casa Anita** (16 C la Felipe, Tel. 972-25-84-71). Small and intimate with barrels of the house wine up on shelves, the seafood is superb, portions are generous, and prices are moderate. Open all year, closed Mondays. No reservations.

Buses to Figueres and Cadaqués leave on a regular schedule from Barcelona's Estació de Nord.

MONTSERRAT

The *Serra de Montserrat* is some 65 kilometers northwest of Barcelona and is the spiritual heart of Catalunya. It's not hard to see why. A series of jagged, bizarre peaks rise dramatically into the air, in a weird and breathtaking formation. Montserrat is a powerful sight at any time, and in particular lights it is wonderous. The peaks have inspired numerous creative artists in and out of Catalunya, including Richard Wagner whose opera *Parsifal* has its roots in Montserrat.

For more than seven centuries, pilgrims have journeyed here to pray at the shrine in the Benedictine monastery, **Monestir de Nostra Senyora de Montserrat** ("Monastery of Our Lady of Montserrat") (Tel. 835-0251). Also here is **La Moreneta** ("the Black Madonna"), a polychrome statue of the Virgin Mary said to date from the 1100s. The sanctuary housing the Virgin in the monastery's basilica is open daily, free to the public, although donations are appreciated. The **Escolania,** a boys' choir, is famous all over Catalunya, and performs each Sunday at 1 P.M. and on occasional holidays. There is also a museum that is open daily.

Apart from these religious sites, the best way to see Montserrat is to take the funicular that goes up a hillside from the monastery. At the terminus of the funicular are numerous paths for walking. Choose one and set out. The views of both the peaks and the surrounding countryside are great. There are also specific paths leading to the cave where the Black Madonna was supposedly discovered, as well as to isolated monks' hermitages.

There are trains from Barcelona to Montserrat, or it is an easy drive in a rental car.

PORT AVENTURA

This is Spain's first theme park. It is located about an hour's drive south of Barcelona on the **Costa Dorada** ("Golden Coast"). North Americans, with their wide experience of theme parks ranging from Disneyland to Busch Gardens to Opryland, may not find this the best they ever visited, but it is a pleasant place to take the kids, with lots of rides—tame and not so tame— and plenty to do. There are five theme areas—Polynesia, the Far West, China, Mexico, and the Mediterranean. Each features rides, a theater for regular stage shows, and stores.

Kids under four are free, between 4 and 12 about 2,500 ptas., and adults pay 4,000 ptas. This entitles you to all the rides and stage shows you want for a day. There is certainly enough to keep most families occupied for that length of time, but if you have done everything to your heart's content and the sun is still out, you can go to the beach less than half a mile away and enjoy some sun and sea. There are numerous day excursions by bus from Barcelona to Port Aventura.

VILAFRANCA DEL PENEDÈS

This is a nice day trip for lovers of the fruit of the vine. An hour southwest of Barcelona, the Penedès region is where Catalunya's fine wines and *cavas* (the Spanish word for champagne) are produced. A number of the best-known vineywards offer tours and tastings, including **Freixenet** (Tel. 891-0700, Fax 891-1254); **Codorníü** (Tel. 301-4600, Fax 317-9678); and **Miguel Torres** (Tel. 890-0100). These phone numbers are all for offices in the city of Barcelona, and there they can provide you with tour hours and tell you how to get there by private or public transport.

RURAL TOURISM

This form of tourism has become increasingly popular in Europe, particularly in the warmer Mediterranean regions. Catalunya, alone, is said to have some 300 places in small villages or in the countryside where you can go to a large farmhouse and have a bedroom and perhaps a bath of your own, and three meals a day, for under 5,000 ptas. a person. If you opt only for breakfast and dinner, the price goes down to nearer 4,000 ptas. This so-called *medio pension* is a good option, because many times there's something to do in the surrounding countryside and you may not want to return for the midday meal.

One of the nicest places for rural tourism in Catalunya is in the pre-Pyrenees region, 60 miles north of Barcelona with its deep pine forests and meadows full of wildflowers in the spring, summer, and fall. The area is laced with hiking trails, including a stretch of the GR trail that goes from France through Spain, somewhat like the Appalachian trail in the United States. There is frequently fishing nearby in rivers or reservoirs. A number of these places are within a half-hour's drive of excellent skiing, both downhill and cross-country.

While you may not share a language with the person running the establishment, the basics of food and lodging are fairly easy to communicate, and most people have no trouble. There are a number of published guides to these places. The Generalitat publishes a good one, in Catalan, which is available from the tourist bureau at 658 Gran Via for 400 ptas. It includes listings as well as photographs of the places.

Glossary

Handy Words in Catalan and Castilian

Catalan	Castilian	English
No parlo català	No hablo español	I don't speak Catalan/Spanish
Carrer	Calle	Street
Avinguda	Avenida	Avenue
Farmàcia	Farmacia	Pharmacy
Sortida	Salida	Exit
Entrada	Entrada	Entrance (or admission ticket)
Esgotar	Agotado	Sold out
Parada de metro	Parada del metro	Metro stop
Muntanya	Montaña	Mountain
Església	Iglesia	Church
Catedral	Catedral	Cathedral
Carretera	Carretera	Highway
Catalunya	Cataluña	Catalonia
Espanya	España	Spain
Espanyol	Español	Spanish
Castellà	Castellano	Castilian

Bitllet	Billete	Ticket (to ride)
Non L'ha	No hay	There is/are not/none
Si us plau	Por favor	Please
Perquè	Porque	Why/because
Gràcies/Mercès	Gracias	Thank you
Socors	Socorro	Help
Perdona'm	Perdoname	Excuse me
Ho sento	Lo siento	I'm sorry
Mira	Mira	Look
Escolta	Escucha	Listen
Caixa	Caja	Cash register
Rebaixa	Rebaja	Sale
Esmorzau	Desayuno	Breakfast
Menjar	Comida	Lunch
Sopar	Cena	Supper
Empenyer	Empujar	Push
Llençar	Tirar	Pull
Aigua	Agua	Water
Pa	Pan	Bread
PSOE	Partido Socialista Obrero de España	Socialist Party
Benzinera	Gasolinera	Gas station
Botiga	Tienda	Store
Lavabo	Lavabo	Bathroom
Bon dia	Buenos dias	Hello; good day
Adéu	Adiós	Goodbye
On	Donde	Where

Sample Menu, Translated

Below is a sample menu. This one comes from L'Hostal de Rita, an inexpensive and nice restaurant in the Eixample.

English
Starter dishes

1. Artichoke omelette
2. Monkfish soup
3. Lettuce hearts with vinaigrette sauce
4. Endives with roquefort cheese sauce
5. Seasonal green salad
6. Sauteed vegetables from Caldes
7. Grilled tender asparagus
8. Chickpeas with pork bits
9. Eggplant pâté
10. White beans with salami from Vic
11. Chicken croquettes with toast
12. Carpaccio (Beef) [raw, marinated, thinly sliced beef]
13. Carpaccio (Tongue) [raw, marinated, thinly sliced tongue]
14. Stewed lentils
15. Chef's macaronis

16. Cod salad (cold) [cod, onions, red peppers in a vinaigrette]
17. Cannellonis Rossini
18. Codfish fritters
19. Codfish crepes
20. Escalibada [baked eggplant, red peppers and onion]

Fish dishes

21. Baby squids sauteed with parsley and garlic
22. Tuna fish baked with tomato
23. Salmon gratin with leeks and carrots
24. Fried codfish
25. Codfish with peppers
26. Monkfish casserole with ripe tomatoes
27. Sole meunière or grilled
28. Baked codfish
29. Grilled sable (white fish)

Meat dishes

30. Beef in red wine from the Ampurdan region
31. Pig's feet
32. Fried brains
33. Beef steak in green pepper sauce
34. Grilled beef steak
35. Roast beef with herbs from Provence
36. Grilled sirloin steak
37. Boiled chicken with vegetables
38. Chicken rolls with ham
39. Baked pig's foot
40. Grilled veal
41. Roasted small chicken
42. Duck with turnips

Desserts

43. Catalan custard with burnt sugar on top
44. Caramel custard with whipped cream
45. Coffee caramel custard
46. Mixed fruit salad
47. Fresh orange juice
48. Ice cream with cookies

49. Ice cream with hazlenuts and toffee
50. Orange ice cream with chocolate
51. Lemon sherbet
52. Raspberry sherbet

Drinks

53. Carbonated mineral water
54. Noncarbonated mineral water
55. Wine
56. Beer
57. Draft beer
58. Espresso coffee
59. Coffee with a splash of hot milk
60. Coffee with hot milk
61. Decaffeinated coffee
62. English tea
63. Mint tea
64. Camomile tea

Castilian (Spanish)
Entrantes

1. Tortilla de Alcachofas
2. Sopa de rape
3. Cogollos a la vinagreta
4. Endivas al roquefort
5. Ensalada verde del tiempo
6. Verduras de Caldes salteadas
7. Parrillada de espárragos tiernas
8. Garbanzos con cansalada
9. Terrina de berenjenas
10. Alubias con miguitas de Vic
11. Croquetas de pollo con tostaditas
12. Carpaccio de ternera
13. Carpaccio de lengua
14. Lentejas estofadas
15. Macarrones de la cocinera
16. Esqueixada de bacalao
17. Canelones Rossini
18. Buñuelos de bacalao
19. Creps de bacalao

20. Escalibada

Pescados

21. Calamarcitos a la plancha con ajo y perejil
22. Atún al horno con tomate
23. Salmón gratinado con puerros y zanahorias
24. Bacalao a la romana
25. Bacalao con pimiento
26. Cassoleta de rape con tomates maduros
27. Lenguado meunier o a la plancha
28. Bacalao a la llauna
29. Mero a la plancha

Carnes

30. Churrasco de buey al vino del Ampurdan
31. Pies de cerdo
32. Sesos a la romana
33. Filete de buey a la pimienta verde
34. Filete de buey a la plancha
35. Rostbeef sobtat a las hierbas de Provenza
36. Entrecot a la plancha
37. Pollo hervido con verduras
38. Rollitos de pollo con jamón
39. Codillo de cerdo a la rapatallada
40. Ternera a la plancha
41. Picantón al estilo de Torroella
42. Pato con nabos

Postres

43. Crema quemada
44. Flan con nata
45. Flan de café
46. Ensalada de frutas
47. Zumo de naranja
48. Helado con galletas
49. Helado con avellana y tofee
50. Helado de naranja con chocolate
51. Sorbete de limón
52. Sorbete de frambuesa

Bebidas

53. Agua con gas
54. Agua sin gas
55. Vino
56. Cerveza
57. Una caña
58. Café solo
59. Cortado
60. Café con leche
61. Discafeinado
62. Té
63. Infusión de menta
64. Manzanilla

Catalan
Entrants

1. Truita de carxofes
2. Sopa de rap
3. Cabdells a la vinagreta
4. Endivies al roquefort
5. Amanida verda del temps
6. Verdures de Caldes saltejades
7. Parrillada d'espàrrecs tendres
8. Cigrons amb cansalada
9. Terrina d'alberginies
10. Monjetes seques amb espurnes de Vic
11. Croquetes de pollastre amb torradetes
12. Carpaccio de bou
13. Carpaccio de llengua
14. LLenties estofades
15. Macarrons de la cuinera
16. Esqueixada
17. Canelonis Rossini
18. Bunyols de bacallà
19. Creps de bacallà
20. Escalibada

Peix

21. Calamarcets a la planxa amb all i julivert

22. Tonyina al forn amb tomaquets
23. Salmó gratinat amb porros i pasanagues
24. Bacallà a la romana
25. Bacallà amb pebrot
26. Cassoleta de rap amb tomàquets madurs
27. LLenguado meunier o planxa
28. Bacallà a la llauna
29. Mero a la planxa

Carns

30. Xurrasco de bou al vi de L'Ampurdà
31. Peus de porc
32. Cervellets a la romana
33. Filet de bou al pebre verd
34. Filet de bou a la planxa
35. Rostbeef sobtat a les herbes de Provença
36. Entrecot a la planxa
37. Pollastre bullit amb verdures
38. Farcellets de pollastre amb pernil
39. Garró de porc a la rapatallada
40. Vedella a la planxa
41. Picantó a l'estil de Torroella
42. Anec amb naps

Postres

43. Crema cremada
44. Flam amb nata
45. Flam de cafè
46. Amanida de fruites
47. Suc de taronja
48. Gelat amb galetes
49. Gelat amb avellana i tofee
50. Gelat taronja amb xocolata
51. Sorbet de llimona
52. Sorbet de gerds

Begudas

53. Aigua amb gas
54. Aigua sense gas

55. Vi
56. Cervesa
57. Cervesa de baril
58. Cafè només
59. Tallat
60. Cafè amb llet
61. Cafè descafeinet
62. Té Anglès
63. Infusió de menta

Index